PSALMS

FOR NORMAL PEOPLE

A Guide to the Most Relentlessly
Theological Book in the Bible

Joshua T. James

The Bible for Normal People Book Series

PSALMS FOR NORMAL PEOPLE

Copyright © 2023 by The Bible for Normal People
Published by The Bible for Normal People
Harleysville, PA 19438
thebiblefornormalpeople.com

Library of Congress Control Number: 2023902617

ISBN: 978-1-7364686-4-7 (Print)
ISBN: 978-1-7364686-5-4 (eBook)

Cover design: Tessa McKay Stultz
Typesetting: Ania Lenihan

For Kate, Abe, and Jude

TABLE OF CONTENTS

Infomercial vii

Section One

1. Psalms from 30,000 Feet. 1

2. The Book of Psalms is Really Old 13

3. We Don't Know Who Wrote Psalms 23

4. The Psalms are Ambiguous. 37

5. The Genres of the Psalms 43

6. The Psalms are Poetic 59

7. Reading Psalms as a Mixtape. 69

Section Two

8. The God(s) of the Psalms 83

9. Sea Monsters & Dragons 91

10. "For Yahweh's *Acts of Faithfulness* Endure Forever" 99

11. The (Still) Costly Loss of Lament 105

12. Did People Really Pray for *That* to Happen? 115

13. In Psalms, God Is a Warrior & That's OK 125

14. Lessons in Being Subversive 135

15. Humanity in Psalms: Somewhere Between Gods & Worms . 141

16. The Psalms & Jesus 155

Conclusion 163

Things for Normal People to Read
(Or Not ... No Judgment) 165

Acknowledgments 167

About this Book 169

Infomercial

Hi. I'm Josh. You probably don't know me, so before we spend 176 pages together, I thought it might be helpful to provide you with one key piece of personal information: I'm a huge Bible nerd. This character trait is most clearly demonstrated by the fact that I have spent an embarrassing portion of my adult life as a student in various formal educational settings with the goal of learning as much as possible about the languages, cultures, peoples, and socio-historical, socio-religious, and geopolitical contexts of the Hebrew Bible.[1] My experience with people has conveyed (in no uncertain terms) that the decision to spend a bunch of money and decades of one's life tucked away in the basement of various theological libraries is an odd career path. I'm going to go out on a pretty sturdy limb and assume that you have taken a

---

[1] For some readers, the traditional Christian designation to describe the first half of the canon, the Old Testament, is problematic. The defining adjective, "old," can denote something irrelevant or inferior or in need of completion—all meanings that work to diminish the collection's role and importance on its own terms. As a result, some prefer the Jewish designation the "Hebrew Bible" or the "Tanak" (an acronym based on the beginning letters of the three sections of the Hebrew Bible: the Torah, the Nevi'im, and the Ketuvim). Others, perhaps attempting to retain a Christian interpretive identity, have proposed the First Testament or the Older Testament as a necessary corrective. Words and intentions matter, so I have a great deal of respect for those wishing to avoid any hint of Christian supersessionism through an adapted use of terminology. In this work, I will use the Hebrew Bible.

different route. You already strike me as the type of person who places a good deal of emphasis on practicality, financial security, and Vitamin D, so the ole PhD in biblical studies probably wasn't in the cards. And yet, despite our differences in background, I bet we are pretty similar. Your preference in reading material, at least, is leading me to believe that you're also interested in all things Bible—its background, its history, its diverse cultural contexts, its theologies and its ethics. Like me, you want to know what this sacred text is all about and whether it's worth the hassle.

If that's the case, then good. I've written this book with someone like you in mind. *Psalms for Normal People* is an introduction to the Hebrew Bible's time-honored collection of ancient Israel's poems, praises, petitions, pleas, and prayers. (Sorry. Occupational hazard. I'm a minister. I'll try to minimize the alliteration from here on out.) In keeping with *The Bible for Normal People*'s overarching goals, I will bring you the best in biblical scholarship—all the terms, ideas, important people, and significant interpretive movements and approaches—so that we can have an honest conversation about what Psalms is, what it's doing in its historical and literary context(s), and how we can read it well.

There is one pretty sizable problem with a book like this. Our biblical source material is massive. Psalms ranks third in the Hebrew Bible in terms of total word count behind Genesis and Jeremiah, respectively.[2] Because of its immense size, I won't be able to go through each composition line by line. (I know. I'm sad too.) I have to be selective, and as a result, I'm sure I'll miss some stuff that might interest you. To help offset any potential disappointment, I've included a list of resources for further study at the end of the book.

What we will discuss falls into two main sections. In chapters one to seven, we'll explore the relevant, seminary-type, introductory issues.

---

[2] If the metric is the most chapters, Psalms would take the gold (though, we would do well to remember that chapter divisions were added much, much later).

The list includes what we know about Psalms' history, date, authorship, and setting; how it was edited and arranged; how it may have been used; how scholars have approached Psalms in the past; and how scholars approach it today. All of this descriptive/historical/literary/interpretive work will be really important because, whether we know it or not, our take on these issues frames how we look at the book as a whole. It is necessary preparatory work. My goal in this first section is to provide us with a good starting point—one that respects Psalms as a collection of ancient poetic literature.

In chapters eight to sixteen, we'll get theological. One of my former teachers says Psalms is the densest theological material in the Hebrew Bible.[3] It's a big claim, but I think he's right. Theology is, quite literally, talk about God. Consider the prayers, litanies and worship songs that are voiced in, say, a modern synagogue or church. They communicate a lot about God because when people pray and sing songs of worship, they are making claims about the type of character their God possesses, what they think their God has done in the past or will do in the future, and all the things that make their God ... well, God. There's a Latin phrase that provides a helpful shorthand for this intersection of belief and practice: *Lex orandi, lex credendi*. The idea is, what you pray is what you believe. As we will soon see, the book of Psalms can be viewed as a worship sourcebook for ancient Israelites. It contains diverse prayers, litanies, and songs for ancient worshipping communities, so by its very nature, the collection offers many and varied theological statements about the God being worshipped. And because these compositions are poetic, there are no long-winded philosophical pontifications, wordy expositions, or lengthy theological treatises. Quite the opposite, in fact. What we have in Psalms is a bunch of terse but still deeply theological prayers and songs.

Despite the book's deep theological undercurrent, I'm not going to try to provide the definitive word on "the" theology of Psalms.

---

[3] See John Goldingay, *Psalms 1–41* (BCOTWP; Grand Rapids, MI: Baker Academic, 2006), 69.

That's impossible. Psalms is way too diverse. We'll unpack this concept throughout the book, but for now, consider Psalms' varied content as a case in point. Sometimes its authors are praising God, sometimes they are screaming at God for being absent, sometimes they are giving thanks for God's deliverance, sometimes they are pointing their fingers at God for not owning up to God's end of the bargain, sometimes they are lamenting or protesting, sometimes they are detailing their experience in the pits of despair, and sometimes, at the end of these stories, things work out, but most of the time we don't know what happens after their prayer is offered. This situational diversity clearly impacts the psalmists' theology.[4] You can't reduce the entire book's message to one thing, as if each writer thought in the exact same way, theologically. (They didn't.) In fact, their answers to the perennial questions posed by people of faith can be quite distinct at times. As a result, it's best if we pick out some theological ideas from certain psalms, without presupposing that these ideas are consistent throughout the entire collection. (They aren't.) The commentary in the second half of the book, then, will function more as a witness to the variety of culturally-embedded theological snapshots included in Psalms. To be sure, all of the book's compositions have been gathered and preserved in this one authoritative collection, which, I think, is important. Despite their theological diversity, maybe even because of their theological diversity, these poems have been approved for use and gathered together.

So there you have it. In this book, I'll introduce you to Psalms, which means we will discuss the foundational background and historical information that guides our reading of its poems and the book as a whole. Then I'll unpack some of what I think are the psalmists' most fascinating theological ideas. In both sections, I'll be as objec-

---

[4] "Psalmist" is the preferred term for an author of a psalm. It's ambiguous, which means we can talk about what the author is doing or saying without feeling any pressure to provide their name. I'll talk about this more in Chapter Three, but the spoiler is, we don't know who wrote the psalms, so this is the safest (and best) option.

tive as I can. I know, I know … objectivity is impossible. I just mean, I don't want to presume that every reader believes Psalms is still relevant today. You might, and it's fine if you do. You wouldn't be alone. Nearly a hundred years ago, Hermann Gunkel characterized Psalms as "perhaps the most frequently interpreted and most beloved book of the Old Testament."[5] I'm not so sure that first claim holds up today,[6] but maybe the second half of Gunkel's description resonates with you: Psalms is and has been your biblical ride-or-die. It offers you a level of familiarity and nostalgia and comfort that is virtually unmatched. I get that. But it's definitely not a prerequisite for what I'm wanting to do here. It's much more important to me that, as readers, we are exposed to Psalms in its ancient contexts and that we observe the various theological commitments of its authors at work in their poetry. It's neither my job nor my intent to convince you to believe all of Psalms' theological claims. As I hope you will soon see, it would actually be pretty weird if you did. The chronological and cultural gap is often too difficult to bridge. I mean, I have an entire chapter on sea monsters in Psalms if that tells you anything (Chapter Nine, if that piqued your interest).

If you're a fan of *The Bible for Normal People*, then I assume you already know this to be true: it's often the case that some attempted objectivity, some historical-critical nerdom, some imposed distance from what might otherwise be a familiar and nostalgic and beloved book will ultimately help us understand it better and appreciate it more fully. That's definitely been my story, and it's my hope for yours, too, regardless of your deep and abiding love (or not) for Psalms.

---

[5] Hermann Gunkel, *Introduction to Psalms: The Genres of the Religious Lyric of Israel*, comp. Joachim Begrich, trans. James D. Nogalski (Macon, GA: Mercer University Press, 1998), 1. Note: We'll talk a lot about Gunkel in what follows. You sort of have to when you're discussing Psalms. Much of what we now take for granted about Psalms—and how to read Psalms—was originally developed by Gunkel around the turn of the twentieth century.

[6] See Brent A. Strawn, *The Old Testament Is Dying: A Diagnosis and Recommended Treatment* (Grand Rapids, MI: Baker Academic, 2017).

Whatever has brought you to this point, where I imagine you sitting in your favorite coffee shop armchair, flavored oat-milk latte and fancy fountain pen in hand, ready to read a book about the Hebrew Bible's preeminent collection of ancient Israel's theologically-infused songs and prayers, I'm glad you're here.

CHAPTER ONE

Psalms from 30,000 Feet

It's a unique feature of *The Bible for Normal People*'s commentary series to include an introductory chapter discussing the book's subject "from 30,000 feet." In some ways, providing a view from this vantage point is a tall task (no pun intended) when it comes to Psalms. In contrast to nearly every other book in the Bible, Psalms does not have an easily identifiable narrative outline, structure or argument, which makes sense: it's not a story or a letter. It's a compilation, an anthology, a boxed-set of an unknown number of ancient Israelite poets' "greatest hits." If you were to glance at its contents and pick out a line here and there, it would probably read like a super-random-poetic-mish-mash (that's a technical term[1]). I'll try to make a case that it's not—that there's something more going on here—but I understand how skipping around from one poem's ecstatic and heartfelt praise to another's gut-wrenching lament might give you emotional whiplash.

One reason for the book's perceived haphazardness is the sheer scope of its included content. An early church ancestor named Athanasius famously concluded, "It is my view that in the words of this book the whole human life, its basic spiritual conduct and as well its occasional movements and thoughts, is comprehended and contained. *Nothing to be found in human life is omitted.*"[2] More than a thousand

---

[1] Jokes.
[2] Athanasius, *Ad Marcellinum* (my emphasis).

years later, John Calvin reached a similar conclusion. Psalms, he says, is "*an anatomy of all parts of the soul*; for there is not an emotion of which any one can be conscious that is not here represented as in a mirror."[3] I tend to think both of these authors are overstating the case a bit. Psalms, for all of its literary artistry and enduring influence, is still heavily embedded within an ancient patriarchal social structure, so I'm a little hesitant to say *nothing* is omitted. But still, their point is well-taken—there's a lot going on in Psalms, and it ranges from the good to the bad to the worse with an appropriate amount of ancient spiritual/ritual/liturgical stuff sprinkled in between.

Another reason reading Psalms can feel disjointed is because of how we approach it. To demonstrate, let me use an example that might land with my people—all of you fabulous 90s kids. There is a tendency to read Psalms in the same way we used to listen to those yearly, mass-produced CD compilations of hit songs by various artists. For reference, think *Now That's What I Call Music* or, if you were a God-fearing Christian whose parents banned "secular" music for fear that you would immediately start having sex and doing drugs, the *Wow* series. (That's a deep cut, isn't it?) If you had one of these CDs in your Discman, you would, no doubt, enjoy some of the songs that were included, but since your listening enjoyment was at the liberty of the record label's producers, there were also a few tracks you immediately skipped. The point wasn't listening to all of the songs in order from start to finish, as if the artists were trying to present a unified message. These collections were popular because, in a world without music streaming services, they gave us quick access to a bunch of our favorite songs on one album.

We can think about Psalms in a similar way. We read some. We skip others. We like some. We don't like others. And because Psalms is a collection of poetry, we give ourselves full license to read whatever

---

[3] John Calvin, *Commentary on the Book of Psalms* vol. I, trans. James Anderson (Edinburgh: Calvin Translation Society, 1843–55; repr., Grand Rapids, MI: Eerdmans, 1948–49), xxxvii (my emphasis).

individual composition we want, in whatever order we want, without fear of missing the book's "point." I have no hard evidence for this, but even if we were inspired to read Psalms in order, from Psalm 1 to Psalm 150, I'm guessing it would still feel somewhat disjointed because of our mindset going in. We intuitively read these poems as self-contained entities, so at the end of each one, we take a breath, turn the page, and along with Ariana say, "thank u, next." As a result, the forest can easily be lost for the trees.

Where my analogy falls apart is, the songs in *Now That's What I Call Music* or the *Wow* series are united by a shared genre: the former is poppy Top 40, the latter is CCM. The content of Psalms is much more diverse. It is a collection of 150[4] of ancient Israel's prayers, petitions, complaints, thanksgivings, and a bunch of other less repeated and, therefore, less familiar poetic forms. Due to the inherent difficulty in describing such a generically diverse collection of poems, some readers prefer to use a catchall that is broad enough to safely encompass all of its content. A popular suggestion is identifying Psalms as "Israel's hymnbook." And indeed, the book's two primary, non-Hebrew titles—"Psalms," and the much fancier/make-you-look-smart-at-a-party alternative, "the Psalter"—suggest, in their native Greek tongue, some relation to singing and music.[5]

---

[4] Following the order of the text in the Hebrew Bible, our English translations contain 150 individual psalms. Some scholars question the legitimacy of the imposed chapter divisions. The structure and content of Psalms 9 and 10, for example, seems to suggest that the two poems were originally one. This is based on the fact that Psalm 10 does not have a title, which is odd compared to most of the psalms around it. (We'll talk more about titles in Chapter Three.) Also, Psalm 9 ends somewhat uniquely with the editorial note, "selah." Both of these oddities suggest the two poems belong together.

[5] You want to get good and nerdy in the footnotes? Nice. Here you go. These two titles—"Psalms" and "the Psalter"—come from two different Greek words. "Psalms" is derived from the Greek word *psalmoi*—a plural noun meaning "songs." It was used to title the book in the Greek translation of the Hebrew Bible (the Septuagint). "The Psalter" comes from the Greek word, *psalterion*, meaning "a stringed instrument" or "a song accompanied by a stringed instrument." It was used as the book's title in the Vulgate, which is the Latin text

Describing Psalms as a hymnbook, however, can be a bit restrictive if you push the label too far. It's not just a collection of songs. It's more of a hybrid volume—a worship sourcebook that includes various elements to be used in a corporate worship setting. It's part old church hymnal (because it does contain songs), part *Book of Common Prayer* (because it also contains written prayers and litanies), and, as I will argue in the next section, part expertly crafted Spotify playlist.

An Ancient Playlist

When you zoom out from the individual psalms, the book provides compelling evidence of *intentional editorial shaping*, like a good playlist. In other words, it's not as haphazard, chaotic and disjointed as it initially feels.

In contrast to the CD compilations I mentioned earlier, my playlists are highly curated (by me) for (my own) specific purposes. There are no skippable tracks. If there were, I'd simply delete them. Each track has been selected. I have some playlists made for running, some that are meant to put me in my feelings, some that help me get safely from Point A to Point B late at night. When I make a playlist, I don't just drag and drop and add the new selection to the end of the list. I arrange the songs. I organize the songs. I shape the songs. At a broad level, Psalms also has a structure, a movement, a mood, a flow. It has an order. It has a shape. According to some, the arrangement of its poems even has a story to tell.

---

tradition. Both of these terms identify the Psalms with singing. The Hebrew title of the book is *Tehillim*, which means "praise(s)." As most commentators point out, this is an odd title given the book's varied content. Praise is only an appropriate description of *some* of Psalms' poems. The ancient Jewish interpretive community knew non-praise psalms existed, of course, so perhaps there is something for us to learn from their resolute use of the title, "praises."

This take might sound novel, but it's not unique to me. It's one of those scholarly advancements that rarely trickles down to everyday, normal readers.

In the 1980s, scholars began to think about Psalms as a *book* or, if you will, as a *playlist*. Instead of focusing on the individual psalms and their hypothetical authors/settings/historical background, they began to consider the editors of the book. The questions shifted from who wrote this psalm and when and why and for what purpose, to who was the master architect, the editor(s) extraordinaire, of ancient Israel's *Wow: Worship* playlist. And what was their story? Was it just one person or was it a few people dragging and dropping their favorite songs into a master playlist? Did the compiler(s) complete the work in one sitting or did it take a while? Did they copy any full albums from their favorite artists and, if so, did they keep the songs in the album's original order? And what about their intent in crafting the playlist? How intentional was the list of songs? Was it random? Was it ordered? Were the compilers trying to create a mood?

We'll talk more about this in Chapter Seven. To prep you, some of the conclusions scholars reach get a little contentious because there is disagreement on *the degree to which* they think Psalms has been intentionally edited. Some folks want to claim every psalm has been put in its proper place for a specific purpose. Others think that's crazy and, much like all of the historical questions people used to ask about individual psalms, impossible to prove. Despite these academic squabbles, there is a surprising amount of scholarly agreement if we stick to the general shape of Psalms, which provides a helpful 30,000-foot view for the book.

The Development and Shaping of Psalms

The version of Psalms we have in our English Bibles took a long time to develop. Noted Hebrew Bible scholar Brevard Childs writes, "It has long been recognized [*and here I should clarify, it has long been recognized *by scholars*] that the present shape of the Psalter reflects a long history of development in both its oral and literary stages."[6] In other words, the entire collection/playlist did not come together overnight. It is the product of many disparate sources—all of those really old, really diverse, theologically dense poems—which were, apparently, continually arranged and rearranged by many editorial hands over a long period of time until the book reached its final form. The ongoing and intentional development of Psalms is based on a number of important observations.

(1) The Presence of Pre-existing Psalm Groups in Psalms

Some psalms appear to have been grouped together *prior to their inclusion* in what we now know as the book of Psalms. These are called "psalm groups." (Note: when given the chance to name something, scholars will usually choose boring.) Childs identifies the "psalms of ascent" (Psalms 120–134), the Asaph psalms (Psalms 50, 73–83), and the Korah psalms (Psalms 42, 44–49, 84, 85, 87, 88) as examples. There is also a group of "David psalms" in Psalms 138–145 that functions in this way. Ostensibly, each of these psalm groups existed on their own as a mini-collection prior to their inclusion in Psalms. Then, at some unknown point later on, they were assimilated into the larger collection.

Using our playlist analogy, you can think of a psalm group as a band's full-length album that has been dragged and dropped into the playlist. The songs had a life and an audience, maybe even a specific structure/order, prior to their inclusion in the playlist.

---

[6] Brevard S. Childs, *Introduction to the Old Testament as Scripture* (Philadelphia: Fortress Press, 1979), 511.

(2) Remnants of Old Edits in Psalms

Another indication of the book's ongoing development is an odd line that appears at the end of Psalm 72. It reads, "The prayers of David son of Jesse are ended" (72:20). This "ending" makes no sense in its current position at the midway-ish point in the book. If you keep reading, you'll soon find that the statement isn't even true. While "David psalms" are much less frequent after Psalm 72, they do continue to show up. What we have in this line, then, is an early "ending" of Psalms that didn't stick. More psalms were added. The book continued to grow. The editorial note in Psalm 72 is like a vestigial organ that provides evidence of the book's continued evolutionary development

(3) An Introduction and Conclusion (and Maybe Some Stuff in Between)

Despite the foregoing, the version of Psalms we have now didn't result from editors simply tacking stuff onto the end of the collection as each new poem was written and accepted for use by the community. The book has been editorially *shaped*. Again, the degree to which this editorial work took place is up for debate. But scholars are nearly unanimous (oddly so) in proposing the intentional editorial placement of Psalm 1 and Psalms 146–150 as the collection's introduction and conclusion, respectively.[7]

Psalm 1, the "playlist's" opener, sets the tone for what will unfold in the rest of the book. Scholars claim it has been placed in this spot on purpose by an editor/editorial team to guide a reading of the whole book.[8] It's like a hermeneutical key to everything that follows.

---

[7] Some add Psalm 2 as part of the book's intentionally placed introduction, too. (For more on that, see the next footnote.)

[8] Nerd note: Viewing Psalm 1 as a proper opener is not due only to the content of the psalm. It is also based on manuscript evidence, some of which includes Psalm 1 without a number or in a different color ink than the other compositions in Psalms. This oddity seems to suggest that Psalm 1 was viewed as a

At the other end, Psalms 146–150 is identified as the playlist's closer. It's like a grand encore … a five-song set that brings the collection to an end in a crescendo of praise. And it, too, seems to be there on purpose. Viewed as intentionally placed bookends, Walter Brueggemann says, the movement from Psalm 1 to Psalms 150 is indicative of a movement within the collection from obedience (a theme in Psalm 1) to praise (Psalm 150).[9]

(4) The Five Books of Psalms

Another indication of intentional editing is the division of Psalms into five "books": Psalms 1–41, 42–72, 73–89, 90–106, and 107–150. (Earlier I referred to Psalms as "a boxed-set of an unknown number of ancient Israelite poets' 'greatest hits.'" Now, I can update the description: it's "a five-disc, boxed-set…") English Bible translations usually acknowledge these divisions at the "seam psalms"—the psalms that begin or end a "book"—with a heading. But, again, because we usually approach Psalms in piecemeal fashion, its five-book structure is often overlooked.

It's not just the existence of these divisions that suggest editorial intention. When you look at the structure of the five books, there is a symmetry between them. The most striking evidence of this is that each book ends with a doxology. And not only that, the content of the doxologies are all very similar. For example, Psalm 41:13 concludes the

---

different sort of composition early on—as a preface, an introduction, something to be read intentionally at the beginning. In addition to the manuscript evidence of the Hebrew text, there is also relevant manuscript evidence in the book of Acts (in the New Testament) to consider. In Acts 13, the author recounts one of Paul's sermons. In it, Paul cites what we know as Psalm 2. Interestingly, some manuscripts identify this psalm as Psalm 1, which suggests that even some of the copyists of the New Testament were working with a text tradition *without* the Psalm 1 that we know.

[9] See Walter Brueggemann, "Bounded by Obedience and Praise: the Psalms as Canon," *Journal for the Study of the Old Testament* (50) 1991: 63–92.

first book with, "Blessed be the LORD, the God of Israel, from everlasting to everlasting. Amen and Amen." The second book ends, "Blessed be the LORD, the God of Israel, who alone does wondrous things. Blessed be his glorious name forever; may his glory fill the whole earth. Amen and Amen" (Psalm 72:18–19). The similarities, which continue in Books 3–5, suggest a unified editorial hand (or hands) behind the addition. In other words, someone/some editorial community thought it would be good to add a similar formal ending to each of the five books to link them together.

Most scholars think Psalms' book divisions were decided at a late stage in the editorial game, and depending on who you talk to, you'll get a different story as to why they ended the books where they did and what the divisions mean for the arrangement of Psalms. Some people think the imposed divisions break the book into scenes of a narrative, moving from the rise and fall of the Davidic kingdom (in Books 1–3) to the reclaimed kingship of Yahweh (in Books 4–5). Others are skeptical. (We'll revisit this in Chapter Seven.)

Where everyone agrees is that the intentional five-fold division was conceived in order to put the Psalter on par with the five books of the Torah. It was an editorial way of saying, "Hey. This thing is really important. Like Moses-level important." As a result, some folks read Psalms as torah, which, in addition to "law," can also mean "instruction" or "teaching."[10] Viewed in this way, the book is instructional. It's meant to teach.

(5) The Flexibility of Psalms in the Dead Sea Scrolls

The earliest manuscript copies of Psalms were found in the late 1940s among the Dead Sea Scrolls, a collection of ancient religious texts dating from about 100 BCE to 100 CE. This cache of texts included

---

[10] A good example of this approach is J. Clinton McCann, Jr.'s, *A Theological Introduction to the Book of Psalms: The Psalms as Torah* (Nashville, TN: Abingdon Press, 1993).

copies of portions of the Hebrew Bible, other religious texts, and community documents, which were transcribed or written by an ascetic community in the geographical region of Qumran on the northwestern shore of the Dead Sea. An astonishing thirty-one copies of Psalms were recovered—far more than any other biblical book among the Scrolls.

For the purposes of our discussion on the editorial shaping of Psalms, it's important to note the copies of Psalms found among the Dead Sea Scrolls didn't preserve the same order of psalms. The variety suggests that the established order of Psalms was still in flux during this time. It also suggests that differing orders of a book that was clearly authoritative within the community was not something to lose sleep over. The collection was still being edited and shaped. And that was OK.

Putting the Pieces Together

If we add all this together, here's what we get: Psalms is a really diverse, editorially shaped collection of ancient Israel's prayers and songs. There's not a whole lot we can say with certainty regarding the historical background of the individual psalms (and that's OK). There's also not a whole lot we can say about the who, when and why of the book's editors. (That's OK too.) But the book, as we have it, suggests that the collection has an intentional introduction (Psalm 1) and conclusion (Psalms 146–150) that serve to frame the book as a whole. In between these bookends, its diverse content is divided into five "books"—a structural device that is meant to connect Psalms to the five books of Moses, perhaps suggesting that it, too, should be read as God's *instruction*.

Admittedly, the view of Psalms is a little fuzzy from 30,000 feet, but these few characteristics, even the acknowledgment of things we *don't know*, should prove to be a helpful enough starting point for the journey ahead.

In what follows, we will zoom in to discuss the individual psalms, where I'll sketch a good approach to reading them (Chapters Two to Six). We will then conclude Section One with a reassessment of the shape of Psalms, this time focusing on the movement and proposed narrative of the book (Chapter Seven). Only then will we explore some of the more interesting and surprising theological themes contained within this diverse collection of ancient Israel's community-approved poems and prayers (the divine council, ancient sea monsters, and graphically violent prayer requests for justice included).

To begin, let me fulfill my unspoken contractual obligation with *The Bible for Normal People* by making a very obvious, but also extremely important, statement about Psalms …

CHAPTER TWO

The Book of Psalms is Really Old

I don't mean to be insulting by offering such an extremely obvious chapter title. I know that you know the book of Psalms is really old. Still, I want to start with a reminder of the book's age because the fact that Psalms is really old has some important corollaries that impact our ability to read it. Here are a few:

- Because Psalms is really old, it was written in *a really old, now-dead language.*
- Because Psalms is really old, it employs *really old literary devices.*
- Because Psalms is really old, it is dependent upon *really old theologies.*
- Because Psalms is really old, it presupposes *a really old view of the world.*

All of the book's extreme "oldness" means we have some interpretive work to do if we want to understand what's going on with its poetry.

Having said that, I should offer a mild disclaimer. You don't need an advanced theological degree to read or use Psalms. It's actually a pretty accessible book, despite the great distance—culturally, chronologically, linguistically, theologically—between modern readers and the ancient poets ... but that is *exactly* why this chapter will prove to be an important starting point. Our perceived familiarity with some of Psalms' images and phrases, maybe even entire poems, can sometimes cause us to misread them. Just like with the rest of the Bible, we must remember to approach Psalms, as Pete Enns and Jared Byas suggest, "through ancient eyes."[1]

A Shepherd's Guide for Those Who Live on a Cul-de-Sac

Let's test this theory with the most popular psalm in the book, Psalm 23. There are important interpretive layers informing its famous opening line, "The LORD is my shepherd," that we miss if we limit the metaphor to our imaginative reconstruction of an ancient agrarian setting. Of course, the image of shepherding immediately brings to mind, for most readers, the protective and provisional characteristics imbued by this line of work. A shepherd was responsible for the safekeeping of the sheep. So too, Yahweh (i.e., the shepherd) protects and provides for the people (i.e., the sheep). The next few lines in Psalm 23 continue the shepherding metaphor in a way that most of us can understand: green pastures, quiet waters, right paths, the shepherd's rod and staff. All that stuff. We get it.

But the image of shepherding also functioned in the ancient Near East as a kingly metaphor. Much like a shepherd who cares for the sheep, the king was to offer his subjects protection and provision. Ezekiel 34 is the most noteworthy example in the Hebrew Bible linking these two concepts together. Israel's and Judah's kings[2] had failed to live

---

[1] See Peter Enns and Jared Byas, *Genesis for Normal People: A Guide to the Most Controversial, Misunderstood, and Abused Book of the Bible*, 2nd ed. (Perkiomenville, PA; The Bible for Normal People Press, 2019).

[2] The kingdom had been split into two by this point—Israel was in the North with its own king, institutions, political alliances, and center of worship, and Judah was in the South.

up to their end of the bargain. They were not shepherding the people well, so Yahweh takes over:

> For thus says the Lord GOD: I myself will search for my sheep, and will seek them out. As shepherds seek out their flocks when they are among their scattered sheep, so I will seek out my sheep. I will rescue them from all the places to which they have been scattered on a day of clouds and thick darkness. I will bring them out from the peoples and gather them from the countries, and will bring them into their own land; and I will feed them on the mountains of Israel, by the watercourses, and in all the inhabited parts of the land. I will feed them with good pasture, and the mountain heights of Israel shall be their pasture; there they shall lie down in good grazing land, and they shall feed on rich pasture on the mountains of Israel. I myself will be the shepherd of my sheep, and I will make them lie down, says the Lord GOD. I will seek the lost, and I will bring back the strayed, and I will bind up the injured, and I will strengthen the weak, but the fat and the strong I will destroy. I will feed them with justice. (Ezek 34:11–16)

With this context informing our reading, the psalm's lead statement, "The LORD is my shepherd," is not just a poetic line describing Yahweh's good, shepherd-like care of the people. It is a statement of kingship, and, honestly, it is not as endearing as we might like. John Goldingay writes, "The image of shepherding is not always a gentle, pastoral one, and it is often a despised occupation."[3] To be clear, Yahweh is not despised in Psalm 23, but the observation concerning the nature of the shepherd's work forces us to consider the harsh realities of divine kingship. Leading a stubborn and stiff-necked people is

---

[3] John Goldingay, *Psalms 1–41*, Vol. 1 of *Psalms* in the the Baker Commentary on the Old Testament Wisdom and Psalms series (Grand Rapids, MI: Baker Academic, 2006), 348.

not easy for the shepherd or comfortable for the sheep. Those green pastures in Psalm 23 sound nice, but the sheep eventually end up in the darkest valley (v. 4). So, too, in Ezekiel's context, Yahweh takes on the shepherding role, but *only* after the failure of the Israelite and Judean kingdoms, both of which had ended in mass destruction and forced exile to foreign empires. As people hearing Ezekiel's words in an uncertain, exilic context anticipated a divine rule, they are still nursing their wounds.

"The LORD is my shepherd" is a rich metaphor that is deeply embedded not just in the theological world of the ancient Near East, but also in the political one. Due to our unfamiliarity with those worlds, the multi-layered meaning of the metaphor is easily missed by modern readers. We go to the sentimental and individualized intonations much too quickly: "The LORD is *my* shepherd. The LORD takes care of *me*. Even though *I* walk in the valley of deep darkness because of whatever *I'm* experiencing right now, *I* will fear no evil for you are with *me*." In this interpretation it's not about kingship or politics. It's about safe-keeping.

This isn't necessarily a bad reading. In fact, it can be quite meaningful. But there's a lot more going on here than a promise of individual protection.

Why You Don't Hear About Sheol at a Funeral

I'll admit it, the contextual re-reading offered above is pretty tame. It adds some important interpretive layers that would have jumped off the page for an ancient audience, but for the most part, it should've been tolerable. Shepherds and kings—nothing too shocking. I'll warn you, though, it can be very disarming when we go beyond a surface reading to reconstruct the world(s) of Psalms. It can complicate our relationship with some of its familiar and nostalgic words. When we (well … I) start messing with them, we tread (ok, fine, it's me, I'm doing this, I'm treading) on dangerous territory.

Here's another example from Psalm 23, and this one might sting a bit.

Psalm 23 is a common funeral text. The reasons for this are relatively clear. The poem claims that God provides, protects, comforts, and is present with God's people, just like a good shepherd. Those are important realities for a grieving community. However, the poem's use in funeral liturgies is also due to the last verse, which on the surface, seems to describe the hope of an eternal dwelling for the people of God (in this case, the deceased). The King James Version reads: "Surely goodness and mercy shall follow me all the days of my life: *And I will dwell in the house of the* LORD *for ever*" (v. 6). The problem is, that's probably not the best rendering of the Hebrew text.

A good alternative translation of the last poetic line in Psalm 23 is, "And I will *return (continually)* to the house of Yahweh *for as long as I'm alive.*"[4] Not "dwell" but "return." Not "forever" but "for as long as I am alive." It's definitely not as funeral-y, and it definitely doesn't seem as hopeful.

Without getting too far into the weeds, the verbal ambiguity in this line is due to the fact that it's difficult to tell the difference between some of the verb forms for "dwell" (*yashav*) and "return" (*shuv*). This is especially the case if one is considering a consonantal Hebrew text (i.e., one without vowels). Some ancient interpreters, most notably the translators of the Greek Septuagint, read against the decision of the scribes who "pointed" (put vowels in) the Hebrew text. The Hebrew reads "and I will return" (from *shuv*). The Septuagint translators went with, "and I will dwell" (from *yashav*). Other than familiarity, there's no good reason to side with the Septuagint's reading, so I've decided to stick with the Hebrew text, and render the verb as "I will return (continually)."

---

[4] Something like this is usually footnoted in a good translation, but the sacred status of "and I will dwell in the house of the LORD forever" renders it pretty difficult to change, even if most people on the translation committee know it's a deficient translation. It's too well-known and too well-loved to remove.

The other proposed change, at least from some English translations, is my preference to swap "forever" with "for as long as I'm alive." This interpretive move helps us see what the psalmist is saying more clearly. When most people read the term, "forever," they envision the scope of the psalm going beyond death. It's as if the psalmist is implying the action of the verb (whichever verb is chosen) is infinite. It doesn't end. Channel your inner Squints Palledorous from the classic 90s film *The Sandlot*: one's association with the house of the LORD (i.e., the temple) lasts "for-ev-er, for-ev-er, for-ev-er." The Hebrew phrase, *le'orek yomim*, translates literally as "for length of days." It's an idiom meaning, "for as long as I'm alive" or "for my whole life." To go back and forth to the temple for one's entire life is what a good Torah-observant Israelite is supposed to do. And the psalmist knows they won't go back and forth to the temple "for-ev-er." You gotta die sometime.

And when you died, ancient Israelites believed you went to a place called Sheol. Sheol is a completely foreign concept to most of us. You can think of it as a perpetual state of non-existence after death. *It's not hell. It's not heaven.* In fact, heaven and hell were not part of their thinking at all; those concepts would develop later. John Walton writes, "We have learned that the Old Testament has no concept of hell, no words for hell, no place for hell in the ideology, and it therefore has no teaching to offer about it."[5]

Neither is Sheol a place of punishment. It's simply the abode of the dead—sadly, the biblical writers don't go into much detail. Here's what we know about the thought process: *everyone* goes to Sheol and *everyone* stays there—good, bad, indifferent, it doesn't matter. When the psalmists bring up Sheol, which they do quite often, they are usually intending something like, "Don't let me go to Sheol *too soon*" or "Don't let me go to Sheol *before my time*." They're basically saying, "Don't let me die yet!" Sheol was the final destination; that was a given. The psalmists, like Billy Joel, grieved when the good died young.

---

[5] John H. Walton, *Old Testament Theology for Christians: From Ancient Context to Enduring Belief* (Downers Grove, IL: IVP Academic, 2017), 264.

In Sheol, you weren't awaiting bodily resurrection. You weren't awaiting anything, really. Bodily resurrection—which is a *really* important concept in the Christian faith—was another late development. In contrast to the concepts of heaven and hell, bodily resurrection *does* appear in the writings of the Hebrew Bible, but not much, and only very late. In fact, the only clear reference to resurrection is in the book of Daniel, which was, on most accounts, the last book of the Hebrew Bible to be written —probably in the 2nd century BCE. The concept of bodily resurrection is absent in the other 99.9999999% of the Hebrew Bible.[6]

So when the psalmist writes, "I will return (continually) to the house of Yahweh for as long as I'm alive," they mean, "I'll go back and forth to the temple my whole life long, and then I'll die and go to Sheol for my perpetual state of non-existence with all the other dead people."

This re-reading might be difficult for some to accept, not just because of their familiarity with the version of Psalm 23 in most major English translations, but also because of our culture's preoccupation with the afterlife, and the implicit rejection in modern communities of faith concerning Sheol as a valid theological concept. I say implicit only because no one that I know of has spent any amount of time actively denying the existence of Sheol. There's no need! Sheol is *that* far removed from our thinking. And yet, here it is, underlying a large portion of thought in the Hebrew Bible. In fact, an awareness of the dominant beliefs about Sheol is key to understanding the import of the psalm. And we often miss it.

This is partly because we are prone to importing *our* theology back onto the pages of the Hebrew Bible. As an interpretive practice, such a move can have disastrous results, especially if we are trying to reconstruct what a psalmist was trying to say. For example, when we expect

---

[6] Some folks include Ezekiel 37 (the story about Ezekiel's vision of the "valley of dry bones"), Isaiah 26:19, and Hosea 6:1–2 as examples of resurrection, but they are focused on the nation of Israel. They also aren't concerned with "the afterlife." Instead, they use resurrection as an image of national restoration after the Babylonian exile.

Psalm 23 to talk about what happens to a person after they die, and even worse, when we expect it to align with how *we* think about the afterlife, we are doomed from the start. We can't just make the quickest and easiest interpretive connection with no added thought. That would be like saying Sir Walter Scott was referring to the internet in 1808 when he wrote the famous line, "Oh, what a tangled web we weave." He clearly wasn't, and we would be wrong to read that meaning back into the poem.

For J. Clinton McCann, all of this means that Psalm 23 might not be the best funeral text. The psalm isn't about dying. It's definitely not about where one goes after they die. That wasn't a relevant (or open) discussion for the psalmist. Their poem is about living. McCann claims, it "puts daily activities, such as eating, drinking, and seeking security, in a radically God-centered perspective."[7] The message of Psalm 23, therefore, was not written to provide comfort about where the deceased are. Rather, it addresses how the rest of us should live everyday.

"Great, You Ruined My Favorite Psalm. Now What?"

Let's recap what we've covered so far. First, the book of Psalms is really old. Second, because of its oldness, we need to read Psalms "through ancient eyes." We will need to close the cultural, chronological, linguistic, and theological gaps between us and the ancients. And honestly, this work might end up complicating our interpretation of a once familiar psalm. It also might problematize some very dear, long-held interpretive conclusions.

It sounds difficult and scary. But when we read a psalm in context, we might find something unexpected, something altogether different from what we first thought. We might find something challenging and beautiful, something that brings meaning in a new way. This recovery

---

[7] J. Clinton McCann, Jr., "The Book of Psalms" in *The New Interpreter's Bible Commentary* (Vol. 3; Nashville: Abingdon Press, 2015), 364.

of the past, when done well, helps us to empathize with the psalmists. It helps us enter into their world and hear their prayers a little more clearly.

I'm convinced that, despite its age, Psalms does not need to be relegated to the past. I'm also convinced that when we are able to hear the psalmists more clearly in their context, some of their themes might resonate with us. So Psalm 23 isn't what you thought, but that's OK. Maybe now, when you read it "through ancient eyes," you will see it in a better light.

CHAPTER THREE

We Don't Know Who Wrote Psalms

When you think about it, suggesting we don't know who wrote Psalms shouldn't be too surprising. We don't know who wrote many books of the Bible—they are often anonymous or pseudonymous.[1] Still, if my proposed uncertainty in the chapter title struck you as odd, I'd guess it's because you had previously heard *David* wrote Psalms. I'd also guess you heard it presented as fact, as if there was nothing left to consider: David wrote Psalms, done deal.

I don't mean to be the bearer of bad news, but there's more to it than that. True, Davidic authorship of Psalms is the traditional teaching. It's been around for centuries, and it didn't come out of thin air. In fact, there are good reasons to associate David with Psalms, the most obvious being his name is all over it! But here's the thing: when you assess the authorship of the book through the lens of historical criticism some pretty substantial interpretive problems arise—even for the parts with David's name on it.

---

[1] "Pseudonymous" means an author wrote them under someone else's name or assumed identity. Ecclesiastes is a good example. The author, identified in the book simply as "Qohelet" (the "teacher"), is posturing as David's son, Solomon: "The words of the Teacher, the son of David, king in Jerusalem" (Ecc 1:1).

Where the "David Wrote Psalms" Tradition Came From

Let's start with a brief rehearsal of where the traditional teaching comes from. There are two main pieces of textual evidence linking David to the psalms.

(1) According to the Bible, David was a really good musician.

In one of the first stories told about David in the Hebrew Bible, he is recruited by King Saul to play the lyre because Saul is tormented by an evil spirit, which was, oh, you know, sent to him by God! (I will trust the author of *Samuel for Normal People* to deal with that fun tidbit.) Seeing his distress, Saul's attendant recommends David for the job because he was known to play the instrument very well. In the ancient world, music was thought to have magical properties, so playing music could calm evil spirits. Saul seems ready to try anything, so he sends for David, and lo and behold, his musical prowess pacifies Saul's anxiety/depression/rage/sadness/bitterness/whatever emotion an evil spirit would elicit in the mind of an ancient reader (1 Sam 16:14–23).

This introductory story sets the tone for the "David as an accomplished musician" trope in the Hebrew Bible, so we are not surprised later on when David sings psalms at various points in the story of his life. He sings after the death of Saul and Jonathan (2 Sam 1:17–27) and after a military victory (2 Sam 22). He also sings his "last words" (2 Sam 23:1–7). The psalm he offers in 2 Samuel 22, in fact, appears in roughly the same form in the book of Psalms (18), thus providing what appears to be a narrative context for the poem. In the book of Chronicles, David is credited with placing Asaph and his line in the tent that housed the Ark of the Covenant so they could sing praises before God (1 Chr 16). All told, these narratives provide the background for viewing David as a musician and for his involvement in Israel's corporate worship.

(2) The Psalm Titles

Of the 150 compositions in the Psalms, 116 of them have titles. If you count them up, or if you just take my word for it, seventy-three of them are specifically identified as psalms "of David."

Let's nerd out for a second and talk some Hebrew. "Of David" is a translation of the Hebrew phrase, *ledawid* (pronounced "le-da-veed"). This is a compound word consisting of the preposition *le* and the proper name, *dawid*. For many readers, past and present, this Hebrew title is interpreted as an indication of authorship: a psalm "of David" is a psalm "written by David." Hold on to that, because I'm going to push against it in a bit. For now, here are some examples to show you what I'm talking about.

> To the leader: with stringed instruments; according to The Sheminith.[2] A Psalm of David. (Ps 6[3])

> To the leader: according to The Gittith.[4] A Psalm of David. (Ps 8)

In addition to the 73 *ledawid* psalms, another 13 psalms have what are called, "long titles." (Remember what I said about scholars being boring.) The long titles are notable for including a proposed historical setting for the composition. They're always about David. They link a psalm to "when David was doing this" or "when David was doing that." For example:

> A Psalm of David, when he fled from his son Absalom. (Psalm 3)

---

[2] No one knows what "The Sheminith" means exactly. I'll discuss it a little later on in the chapter.

[3] The psalm titles are treated as verses in the Hebrew text, and are therefore numbered "1." English Bibles don't do that. That means that sometimes there will be a discrepancy between the verse numbers in Hebrew and English.

[4] No one knows what "The Gittith" means either. I'll talk about it later in the chapter.

> A Shiggaion[5] of David, which he sang to the LORD concerning Cush, a Benjaminite. (Ps 7)

The other long titles are found in Psalms 18, 34, 51, 52, 54, 56, 57, 59, 60, 63, and 142.

These two strands of tradition—David as a musician and the various references to him in the psalm titles—led many readers in the history of Jewish (and Christian) interpretation to associate David not just with the psalms that bear his name, but with the entire book.

The Tradition of Davidic Authorship—From psalms to Psalms

One of the most straightforward examples of the growth of the "David wrote Psalms" tradition comes from the Greek translation of the Hebrew Bible. The Septuagint's translators, seemingly arbitrarily, increased the number of *ledawid* psalms from 73 to 85. This addition demonstrates that the text was "fluid" (meaning it was open to additions) and the tradition about David writing Psalms was growing.

The Dead Sea Scrolls provide another important reference point in the growing tradition of the Psalms' supposed Davidic authorship. The Dead Sea Scrolls, remember, are a collection of texts dating from about 100 BCE to 100 CE—well after the time of David. In one text, known as the "Psalms Scroll," David is said to have composed 3600 psalms. Yale Hebrew Bible scholar John J. Collins writes, "By the time the Dead Sea Scrolls were written in the first century B.C.E., it was possible to refer to 'David' in the same context as Moses and the prophets to indicate an authoritative body of Scripture."[6] As an authorial figure,

---

[5] Finally, a "Shiggaion," that one's easy. Nah. I'm kidding. No one knows what it means either. But we'll talk about it later in the chapter.

[6] John J. Collins, *Introduction to the Hebrew Bible*, 3rd ed. (Minneapolis: Fortress Press, 2018), 496.

David was not limited to the *ledawid* psalms. By this time, he was associated with the entire book.

A similar attribution is evidenced in a rabbinic source known as the Jewish Talmud. Tractate *b. Baba Batra* identifies David as the author of the "Book of Praises." Another rabbinic source, the Jewish Midrash, reached the same conclusion on the Psalms' authorship.

As we will see, the New Testament also identifies David as the author of the book of Psalms, referring to it inclusively as "the Psalms of David." This conclusion should not be at all surprising given the situatedness of early Christian teaching in the Jewish interpretive tradition.

In one story, Mark has Jesus citing Psalm 110. When he does, he introduces it with a note of Davidic authorship. Mark 12:35–36 says, "While Jesus was teaching in the temple, he said, 'How can the scribes say that the Messiah is the son of David? *David himself, by the Holy Spirit, declared,*

'The Lord said to my Lord,
"Sit at my right hand,
until I put your enemies under your feet."'

Psalm 110 is a *ledawid* psalm, so it has a textual "hook" linking it to David. Other New Testament texts, however, also attribute untitled psalms to David. For example, the author of Acts depicts a group of Jesus followers giving thanks to God following the release of Peter and John from prison. In their prayer, they cite a portion of Psalm 2, which is an untitled psalm, but they introduce it with, "David said..." (Acts 4:25). The author of Hebrews does something similar. They attribute Psalm 95, another untitled psalm, to David (Heb 4:7). These examples, though few in number, indicate a general acceptance of the tradition of Davidic authorship for the entire book (or at least, a large enough portion to warrant associating him with the whole collection).

David Definitely Didn't Write *All* of the Psalms

If we come at the conversation of the authorship of Psalms from a his-torical-critical perspective, however, the conclusion that David wrote the entire book is simply untenable. For starters, there is clear textual evidence in Psalms that some of its poems go well beyond David's time. Psalm 137 begins,

> By the rivers of Babylon—
> there we sat down and there we wept
> when we remembered Zion. (v. 1)

For most scholars, the psalm's introductory line is a dead giveaway of its earliest possible historical setting. By mentioning Babylon and hint-ing at the destruction of Zion (which is basically a codeword for Jerusa-lem), the psalm is best read as an exilic text, meaning, it was written in the aftermath of the Babylonian exile in the 6th century. For reference, David would have been king around 1000 BCE. So either David was writing prophetically (which is a stretch for a number of reasons, but especially since the text appears to be referring to past events) or this psalm was written much later. The latter is clearly a much more logical conclusion.

Another argument against the Davidic authorship of the entire book is the fact that Psalms does not link *all* of its individual composi-tions with David. Only 73 of the titles in the Hebrew text are *ledawid* psalms (85 in the Greek tradition). Other compositions make explicit connections with non-Davidic figures such as Moses (Ps 90), the sons of Korah (Pss 42, 44–49, 84–85, 87–88), Asaph (Pss 50, 73–83), Ethan (Ps 89), Solomon (Pss 72, 127), and a "poor man" (Ps 102). These psalms utilize the same Hebrew word construction as when David is in the title: the preposition *le* + a noun/proper name. If someone inter-prets *ledawid* as an indication of authorship, they would have to say the same thing for whoever else is listed, which means, David didn't write the whole collection.

A Psalm of/to/for/on behalf of/inspired by/concerning/about/dedicated to/belonging to David

Despite the traditions, the fact that David didn't write all the psalms is pretty obvious. But even the psalms that bear his name are a bit more ambiguous than we might suspect. As I've already mentioned, if a title identifies a psalm as "a psalm of David," many readers tend to think that means David wrote the psalm. But there are a few problems with that conclusion.

First, the majority of scholars do not read *ledawid* as an indication of authorship. The construction could just as easily mean a psalm *to David*, a psalm *for David*, a psalm *on behalf of David*, a psalm *inspired by David*, a psalm *concerning/about David*, a psalm *dedicated to David*, a psalm *belonging to David*. The title is a lot more ambiguous than we tend to think. Some good translations choose to reflect this ambiguity by interpreting the phrase: "David's." It's related to him somehow, but the relationship is left open.

Who Is "David" Referring to Anyway?

Second, it's not clear who "David" is referring to. The name has meanings in the Hebrew Bible other than "David, son of Jesse, king of Israel." The referent in a psalm "of/to/for/on behalf of/inspired by/concerning/about/dedicated to/belonging to David" is more ambiguous than we might think.

In Ezekiel 34:23–24, Yahweh says, "I will set up over them one shepherd, *my servant David*, and he shall feed them: he shall feed them and be their shepherd. And I, the LORD, will be their God, and *my servant David* shall be prince among them; I, the LORD, have spoken." Ezekiel is an exilic text, written in the shadow of the Babylonian exile: for Yahweh to say, "I will set up over them one shepherd, *my servant David*" is weird because David would have been dead for four-ish centuries by this time. In this passage, it must be a new "David," a future "David," who will be placed on the throne. Ezekiel is not referencing the old *King David*, as if Yahweh would raise him from the dead (remember, the concept of resurrection hadn't really developed yet). The prophecy must be talking about *a different David* altogether. Sure, the two are linked—the old and the new—but there's a nuance in this passage that we must attend to: who are we talking about here?

We'll discuss the date of Psalms in a later chapter, but it was completed, at the very earliest, *after the exile*. That doesn't mean that all of its poetry was that late, but it does mean that for some readers, the question, which David is being referred to in the *ledawid* psalms, was a real one. Was it the old David (who died a long time ago) or a future David?

The Titles (and other Notations) are about *Function*

To review, the meaning of *ledawid* is ambiguous and the identification of "David" is unclear. Those are the first things to note in this weighted argument against Davidic authorship.

Third, the majority of scholars believe the titles are late editorial additions. They aren't bylines penned by the original author of the psalm. Someone, somewhere, at some later point in time added the titles, including the *ledawid* titles.

Why? The weird words and phrases included in the psalm titles—maskil, the Sheminith, the Gittith, a Shiggaion, according to Muth-labben, according to the Deer of the Dawn—are helpful here. If you read the footnotes, you already know the bad news: no one knows exactly what any of these terms mean, but scholars are in virtual agreement that they are musical notations of some sort. And that has led scholars to conclude that individual psalms were meant to be performed or sung or prayed *in worship*. This is also why so many titles include a note to "the director." The title is not about authorship, it's an instruction to the ones leading the worshipping community on how to use the Psalms *in corporate worship*.

The titles provide directions like, sing the psalm in this key, use this tune for the melody, these are the instruments to be featured, put the capo on the second fret, or even, this one is a "David psalm" (whatever that entails). These directions provide some clarity on the function of the psalms, which is what influenced editors to include notes on how and when the psalms should be performed. In the history of interpretation, clarifying this has been really important. It tells us the psalms were meant to be performed, to be sung, to be used … *in worship*.

David Wasn't Doing *This* or *That* When the Psalms Were Written

Finally, the 13 long titles. There's no ambiguity here. They were clearly about *King David*. They link these poems to specific events in David's life. But again, most scholars have concluded the psalms were not *actually written* when David was doing whatever the title says he was doing. The titles were late additions, which means, they don't provide an accurate historical framework for the poem.

Just like the other titles, the long titles are there to guide the function of the psalm, *hermeneutically*. That doesn't mean they don't also have performative/musical instructions. Some do. It just means the long titles are, more fundamentally, instructions on how to read a psalm. They say, "Think about this event in David's life when you are reading/singing/praying the psalm."

Here's an example of how this might have worked. Say someone in a position to make notes on Psalms (an editor, for instance) reads the psalmist's confession in Psalm 51. It is moving and vulnerable, and it expresses the weight of one's sin. The editor thinks, "Oh wow. This confession reminds me of the story of David and Bathsheba, when Nathan the prophet went and told David what's up. I'll make a note. That could be an interesting intersection for people to consider." The editor (not the author) then ties the psalm to this story in David's life for added context: *To the leader. A Psalm of David, when the prophet Nathan came to him, after he had gone in to Bathsheba.*

The long title is not a historical note—as if the editor were providing necessary background information on the psalm's when, why, and by whom it was written. That's not the point. It's a guide to reading, added to help future singers/pray-ers/worshippers approach and apply the psalm. It's saying, maybe you can use the psalm in a situation roughly equivalent to this David story.

One thing that has led scholars to conclude the long titles are not historical notes (and they were added later) is the fact that when you compare the details in the psalms and the narratives of David's life recorded in the books of Samuel, they don't always line up. For example, the line in Psalm 51 that says, "Against you [God], you alone, have I sinned," rings a little hollow when you consider the larger story of David and Bathsheba. David has just raped Bathsheba (because, really, what can a woman in the ancient world say when the king sends men to "get you" so he can "take you"). Once Bathsheba is found to be pregnant, David then kills her husband, Uriah, by sending him to the front line. Certainly David's sins affected both Bathsheba and Uriah in some really obvious ways, right? It's not just "God alone" he sins against. He's actually left quite a few in his wake who would have (if they were alive) a pretty big bone to pick with him.

What Do We Do Now?

When you put all of this together, the scales tip pretty heavily against the Davidic authorship of the book of Psalms. Some of the obvious issues are the compositions in the Psalms that reflect a time much later than David's life and the psalms that don't identify David as the author. To say he didn't write *all* of them should be easy to accept. But did David write any of the psalms? It's definitely not as clear as we tend to think.

The *ledawid* psalm titles are problematic—they are ambiguous in how the psalm is related to David, it's hard to know which David is being referred to, and they are most likely late additions to the text. In the case of the long titles, we can add another layer arguing against David as the author, namely, the conflicting information between the psalms and the narratives from where they are claimed to derive.

Further, all of the weird stuff in the titles, the supposed musical notations for instance, suggest they were added later and that they are primarily interested in the psalm's function or use. They are not bylines by the psalm's author.

We are left to conclude that there is nothing *in the text* that demands Davidic authorship of any of the Psalms, and, quite honestly, there is not a whole lot to be gained by forcing the issue. Goldingay writes, "It's best to assume we know nothing about who wrote the Psalms, and that this knowledge is unnecessary to using them..."[7] Communities of faith can still sing the Psalms, they can still pray the Psalms, they can still enact or embody or perform the Psalms. They can scream them, chant them, cry them, read them responsively, meditate on them. In other words, even if we don't know who wrote the Psalms, we can still use them.

I'd also add, we can still mine the Psalms for information on ancient Israel's worship practices and theological commitments and the form and structure of biblical Hebrew poetry. We do not need to identify an author to illuminate any of those pursuits.

"You're Forgetting Jesus"

Here's my thesis: it is impossible to know who wrote Psalms. For some of you, my agnosticism on the issue may seem like a direct attack on Jesus, or more accurately, Mark's depiction of Jesus. As I mentioned

---

[7] John Goldingay, *An Introduction to the Old Testament: Exploring Text, Approaches & Issues* (Downers Grove, IL: IVP Academic, 2015), 299.

earlier, Jesus identified David as the author of Psalm 110 according to the Gospel of Mark. How then can I say I don't know who wrote *any of the psalms*? Mark's Jesus said David wrote Psalm 110. So that puts us on pretty solid ground, right?!

Well, I think there is a little more to it …

First, it is not at all clear that Jesus himself said all the things that the Gospel writers say he said. This isn't an attack on Jesus or the Gospels, rather, it is a recognition that the Gospels have a complex compositional history and they include contradictory elements between them. Their authors have clearly shaped their retellings for certain theological purposes. They are not objective historical reports. As a result, the Gospels probably don't always reflect what Jesus *actually* said. The Gospel writers *interpreted* what Jesus said for the benefit of their audience and for their own theological purposes. With this in mind, the majority of New Testament scholars would say the issue is definitely not as simplistic as "If it's in Mark (or any of the other three Gospels), then Jesus must have said it exactly as it is presented."

I realize this first point is opening a massive can of worms, which, thankfully, we don't need to solve here. In fact, for the sake of the argument, let's defy mainline biblical scholarship and pretend the historical Jesus definitely said David wrote Psalm 110. I still don't think that seals the authorship deal.

From what we have seen, no one in the first century would have questioned David's authorship of Psalm 110. Not only was it a *ledawid* psalm, but the association between David and the Psalms was baked into the context. The Septuagint, the Dead Sea Scrolls, the Jewish Talmud and Midrash, and even other portions of the New Testament, all provide clues to this contextual reality. People in Jesus's time spoke about David and Psalms in the same way they spoke about Moses and the Pentateuch (the first five books of the Hebrew Bible). Both were viewed as the authorial figures associated with their respective texts— "the Psalms of David" and "the books of Moses." But the authorship of Psalms and the authorship of the Pentateuch face serious challenges when placed under the lens of historical criticism.

So with regard to Mark's version of Jesus, we have three interpretive options:

1. Jesus was right, and I'm wrong—David wrote Psalm 110.
2. Jesus was wrong, and I'm right—David did not write Psalm 110.
3. "Rightness" and "wrongness" aren't really the best categories because Jesus and his biographer were simply appealing to a well-known tradition.

I'm inclined to go with option three, and not just because it gets Jesus and me off the hook.

I know it *seems* like a clear enough affirmation of authorship, but Jesus wasn't making a case for the Davidic authorship of Psalm 110 in Mark. I would argue that he was speaking conventionally. Saying, "as David says" (or some other related phrase) before introducing a psalm would have been nothing more than a cypher for "as we read in the book of Psalms." Jesus is appealing to Psalms, and he is being depicted as using language that would have made sense to his audience. Since Psalms were "the Psalms of David," why not attribute an individual psalm—*any* individual psalm, let alone a *ledawid* psalm—to David? That's fair game. To claim Jesus is making a statement of authorship, though, is demanding a bit too much from this standard, first century introduction.

It is better to view Jesus as a man of his time—one who, if he really said something about David writing Psalm 110, was simply appealing to a well-known tradition to introduce a selection from Psalms.

For some of you, this may be a lot to take in. It may seem like I am privileging historical criticism over Jesus, but I don't think that's the case. Scholarship has provided many good reasons for us to understand *ledawid* in Psalms differently than the tradition, and it is important for us to listen and weigh its case.

At the end of the day, I think we're safe to claim, we don't know who wrote Psalms.

CHAPTER FOUR

The Psalms are Ambiguous

The same conclusion that I reached regarding the authorship of Psalms—that is, we don't know who wrote it—could stand in for many other historical-critical issues of the book as well. This is especially the case when we are thinking about the background of the Psalms' individual compositions. For instance, we don't (and, I'd say, can't) know a lot of details about a psalm's date of authorship or historical setting or intended use, at least, not beyond a broad claim about its potential use in ancient Israelite worship. The specifics are really fuzzy.

This, of course, does not mean we are unable to say *anything*. As I've already mentioned, some psalms include a thinly veiled reference to their earliest possible historical setting, like the implied reference to the Babylonian exile in Psalm 137. We know that the psalm was not completed before this tragic event, even if we can't narrow down its precise date (i.e., how long *after* 586 BCE it was written). References like this also provide an important hook for dating the final version of the book of Psalms. Since exilic/post-exilic psalms are included in the book, we know it could not have been completed before then.

Information like this is helpful, but it's rare. More often than not, we aren't provided with much to aid our quest for historical context. And here's why—the content of Psalms' poems tends to be ambiguous.

Ambiguity in Psalms

Ambiguity in psalms is a good thing, in that it allows a 2500ish-year-old collection of poems to remain useful for modern readers. This isn't just good news for us. The content of psalms has always been ambiguous and that has *always been* good news. In fact, you could say they have always had to be ambiguous due to the book's function as a communal resource: a communal prayerbook/a communal songbook/a communal worship sourcebook. If Psalms' prayers were overly specific (which, a bit frustratingly, would be helpful in answering our nagging historical-critical questions), then they would be too exclusive, and thus, not very useful for the larger worshipping community.

Here's an example. If a worship leader in a modern church was leading a prayer of confession that got a little too specific—let's say they started asking forgiveness for some very personal, very unique-to-them sins, but framed them in the first-person plural ("we")—not only would it be weird, but it wouldn't be applicable either. It's one thing to say, "Forgive us, Lord, for our tendency to be drawn away from you," and an entirely different thing to provide specific examples of how and when and why and with whom we were drawn away.

Psalm 32 provides an example of how the book's necessary ambiguity works in action. This composition is one of the seven so-called penitential psalms, also known more generally as a psalm of confession. The psalmist writes,

> Happy are those whose transgression is forgiven,
>   whose sin is covered.
> Happy are those to whom the LORD imputes no iniquity,
>   and in whose spirit there is no deceit.
> While I kept silence, my body wasted away
>   through my groaning all day long.

For day and night your hand was heavy upon me;
    my strength was dried up as by the heat of summer.
Selah[1]

Then I acknowledged my sin to you,
    and I did not hide my iniquity;
I said, "I will confess my transgressions to the LORD,"
    and you forgave the guilt of my sin.
Selah (vv. 1–5)

Clearly, there was a specific context informing the psalmist's prayer. Something—a sin of some sort—occasioned their request for divine forgiveness. But what was it? We don't know. The psalm is too vague. On the basis of the text alone, it is impossible to reconstruct what happened. What does it mean that the psalmist's body was wasting away? Or what about the LORD's hand being heavy upon them? We aren't told. We only know the psalmist acknowledged their transgressions (whatever they were), and they were forgiven.

Much like our hypothetical worship leader, if the psalmist went into too much detail, it would prohibit the future use of the prayer in a communal context. When I pray Psalm 32 now, I can easily place myself into the role of the unnamed "I" (the speaker, the pray-er) precisely because the psalm allows me the space to do so. I don't need to know who wrote it. I don't need to reconstruct its historical setting. I don't need to know the date. And I don't need to know what sin is being described in its poetic lines. In fact, all of these things might cloud my attempted use of the psalm if I knew what they were. As

---

[1] Despite the popular teaching that *selah* is an instruction to be silent/to meditate/to enter into a holy pause, no one actually knows what the term means. Goldingay offers this tongue-in-cheek conclusion, "The best theory is that [*selah*] was what [the psalmist] said when he broke a string. This is the best theory because there is no logic about when you break a string, and there is no logic about the occurrence of 'selah'" (*An Introduction to the Old Testament*, 297).

it stands, when I pray Psalm 32, I become … the "I." I become the "speaker." I become the "pray-er." Because of the psalm's ambiguity, I can insert my own sins, I can admit my own transgressions, and I can trust in God's forgiveness of me. The words of this ancient prayer become my own, and my community's, which is precisely how the psalm was meant to function.

Take another example: prayers for healing. Again, our oversharing, overly specific, and just downright awkward worship leader begins a communal prayer for healing, "Lord, you are the healer. We pray for those who are sick in our community, and especially for those who have suffered compound fractures, breaking both the tibia and fibula in their right leg, and who, as a result of post-surgical complications, have incurred an infection of flesh-eating bacteria that will not only inhibit their potential return to the NFL but may also result in the loss of a limb or potentially, their life."

It's a great prayer, and one I'm sure many football fans in the DC metro area offered late in the fall of 2018 as the Washington Commanders' starting quarterback, Alex Smith, suffered a gruesome leg injury. (Do not YouTube this injury.) But this prayer (you want to YouTube it, don't you? I'm telling you, don't do it), despite its merits, is pretty exclusive to Alex Smith. Alright, it's very exclusive to Alex Smith. (You watched it. I warned you. It's brutal, isn't it?) Even if you have someone in your congregation with a broken leg, chances are it will not inhibit their return to the NFL. And if it does, chances are they won't experience a rare flesh eating bacteria as a result of post-surgical complications! As a result, it was a great prayer for Alex Smith … in 2018 … but it's no good for *communal* application. It's too specific.

Again, the book of Psalms seems to get this nuance and, perhaps as a result, eschews specificity in its prayers for healing. Psalm 6 is such a prayer. It begins,

> O Lord, do not rebuke me in your anger,
>   or discipline me in your wrath.
> Be gracious to me, O Lord, for I am languishing;

O LORD, heal me, for my bones are shaking with terror.
My soul also is struck with terror,
    while you, O LORD—how long? (vv. 1–3)

As far as context is concerned, there is not a lot to go on here. The psalmist prays for divine healing as opposed to rebuke and discipline. They are languishing. Their bones are shaking with terror (or shaking in dismay). This bodily response could be metaphorical or literal. It's hard to say. From our reading of the psalm, we can't identify either the source of the affliction or the nature of the requested healing, but again, that is a good thing for the potential communal use (and re-use) of the psalm.

See How Lucky We Are?

I know it's disappointing that we don't know more about the history of the book of Psalms or its compositions, but I'm telling you, it's a good thing. A VH1 "Behind the Music" special on Psalms might ruin everything. The unnamed "I" in the psalms' poetry is not meant to be understood as a historically reconstructable David or Moses or Solomon or Korah or any of the other figures that appear in the titles. Even the long titles want you to go beyond David. The "I" of the psalms is better viewed as a stand-in for an ancient worshipper—*any* ancient worshipper—which allows it to function as a stand-in for *modern* worshippers, too.

Think about the well-known Christian hymn, "I Surrender All." It was written by Judson W. Van DeVenter, who, in the original composition, functions as the "I" surrendering all to Jesus. But when people (who are not Judson W. Van DeVenter) sing the song in a congregational setting, they aren't thinking about the writer. *They* become the "I." They are surrendering all. It's the same with Psalms. Contemporary readers can continue to pray these prayers and sing these songs in a meaningful way *today*, some two and a half millennia removed, because the psalm isn't overly specific.

The specific historical setting standing behind a psalm is relatively unimportant for its continued use. Taken together, Psalms does construct an image of the *type* of people who would pray such prayers and *when* they might pray them and for *what purpose*—but we are still left grasping at straws in our attempted historical reconstructions.[2] It's clear enough that reconstructing this information, in its precise detail, is unnecessary for Psalms' use in corporate worship ... and since we don't have much of this information to speak of anyway, that's a good thing.

---

[2] See Rolf A. Jacobson and Karl N. Jacobson, *Invitation to the Psalms: A Reader's Guide for Discovery and Engagement* (Grand Rapids, MI: Baker Academic, 2013), 95–98.

CHAPTER FIVE

The Genres of the Psalms

To review where we've been up to this point, what we have in the book of Psalms is a collection of ancient Israel's very old, very diverse, very dense, theological poems. We don't know who wrote them or when they were written (for the most part) or what specific events were happening in the life of the psalmist to inspire them. That's largely because these poems are notably ambiguous—they have to be, in order to be useful in corporate worship, which most scholars think was the point. Too much specificity would render these compositions practically unusable by a worshipping community because a pointed and overly specific prayer wouldn't reflect anyone else's "praise," "lament," "sin," "thanks," or "sickness." The one element featured in many psalms (115 of them) that could yield some *potential* historical information is the titles, but, as we've seen, they aren't reliable witnesses. All told, it's pretty bleak from a historical standpoint. What we have is the text in front of us, and that's about it.

So how does all of this affect the scholarly study of the book? Well, for a long time, it didn't. In the 18th and 19th centuries, Psalms scholars focused their attention and resources on the attempted reconstruction of all the classic line-items featured in historical-critical research. That's just what you did in biblical scholarship at this time, even if it meant guessing wildly. As you now know from our brief foray into this world, such attempts ultimately proved fruitless ... which led to an impasse in Psalms scholarship ... which set the stage for the work of Hermann Gunkel (1862–1932).

Gunkel's work on Psalms was groundbreaking. He rejected the dominant interpretive model of his day—namely, the aforementioned attempt to reconstruct the historical background of an individual psalm—because he knew it was impossible. Instead, he pioneered a new way to approach Psalms based on an assessment of a psalm's literary genre and its social setting (in German, its *Sitz im Leben*, "setting in life"). Gunkel's proposal carried the day throughout the twentieth century, and in many ways, Psalms scholarship is still largely dependent upon Gunkel's hundred-year-old advances.

Hermann Sorts Your CDs

We'll get to the psalm's social setting in a bit. First, let's think about genre. To start, let me give you an analogy that will hopefully explain what Gunkel did and how he revolutionized our understanding of the literary genres represented in Psalms.

Do you remember going to a music store to buy CDs? It's a dated example, I know, and honestly, the medium doesn't matter. Insert cassette tapes, 8-tracks, or records in place of CDs if need be. Whatever the case, most music stores had all their albums organized on racks in alphabetical order and according to musical genre. I doubt we considered this, but behind the scenes, a dutiful employee would have been tasked with the organizing and shelving of the store's weekly shipment of new products, so that if a customer was looking for, oh I don't know, the hit single, "Wannabe," by a group of zany British pop stars called, "The Spice Girls," back in 1996, then that person would know exactly where to find it. (This example, by the way, is totally hypothetical. I'm definitely not talking about my 14-year-old self, Orange Julius in hand, making a beeline to the "Top 40" section in my local Sam Goody's music retailer.)

In this analogy, Gunkel is the dutiful music-store employee, organizing the inventory on the racks under their proper genre category so you and I can find them, buy them, and enjoy them ... except for this analogy to work, Gunkel was given a box of unlabeled and unfamiliar records by unknown artists spanning many unknown genres. He had to listen to them, study them, define all their musical traits, categorize them, make up a bunch of different genres, get a label-maker and print out the genre categories he made up, put the labels on the racks in the store, and then sort the music accordingly.

Praise, Lament, Thanksgiving, Etc.

It should be obvious, but it needs to be said, identifying the genre of a psalm, even with Gunkel's groundbreaking work in the rearview mirror, is much harder than identifying the genre of a song on the radio. We can do the latter intuitively because of our level of familiarity with diverse musical genres. When we press the scan button on our car radios on a road trip, we get a snippet of a song, but within three seconds of hearing it, we can recognize the genre and know whether or not we want to keep listening. That's because we are familiar with how chord progressions, vocal runs, lyrical cadences, bass lines, electric guitar tones, and other musical elements work within a given genre.

Categorizing psalms, on the other hand, puts us quite literally in foreign territory. It's done based on a psalm's *form* and *content*—and again, we are largely unfamiliar with the form of a psalm's genre (how it is ordered or structured) and its content (what types of things a psalm says in a certain genre). Yet again, there are notable cultural, chronological, and linguistic gaps between us and the ancient Near East that complicate the matter.

Still, whatever difficulties we face now, Gunkel had it much worse in the early twentieth century. When he started his categorization project, there was no existing catalog of psalm genres available to him. He wasn't mindlessly filing various psalms onto racks that already had genre labels affixed. He had to become familiar enough with the Psalms' material that he could identify and categorize the psalms himself!

To accomplish this organizational task, Gunkel devoured the diverse poetry of Psalms and any other poetic material in the Hebrew Bible. This list includes the poems embedded in the narratives, e.g., the "Song of the Sea" in Exodus 15, Hannah's prayer in 1 Samuel 2, and Jonah's thanksgiving in the belly of the fish in Jonah 2. It also included the overwhelming majority of the book of Job, which is a massive, 39-ish chapter, poetic dialogue, and the "psalm-like elements" in Israel's prophetic texts.[1] Gunkel also gathered examples of poetry from outside the Hebrew Bible. As archaeological finds began to pile up in the early twentieth century, Gunkel scoured non-biblical texts from the Apocrypha (a collection of Jewish writings from the Second Temple period) and other poetic texts from many newly discovered Babylonian, Assyrian, and Egyptian sources. As a result of his deep dive into ancient poetic literature, Gunkel began to see patterns emerge in the form and content of the poetry in Psalms. His observation of these recurring formal literary characteristics—how a poem moved, its structure, what elements it included and when they appeared—and themes (its content), led to the creation and, eventually, the categorization of genres in Psalms.

Gunkel identified five main genre categories: hymns (or praise psalms), royal psalms, communal laments, individual laments, and thanksgiving psalms. He also identified a bunch of minor genres, too, such as pilgrimage songs, victory songs, communal thanksgivings, legends, torah psalms, and sayings of blessing and curse. We should think of the descriptive adjective, "minor," in terms of the genre's frequency, not its importance. All of the genres, regardless of how often they occur, are important, as is identifying them properly. In fact, Gunkel concluded that genre analysis is "nonnegotiable."[2] If we misidentify a psalm's genre, we will probably misunderstand its message.

---

[1] Gunkel, *Introduction to Psalms*, 3.
[2] Gunkel, *Introduction to Psalms*, 5.

Over the years, scholars have tweaked Gunkel's genre categories. It is common for his five genres to be reduced to *three*—praise, lament, and thanksgiving. Another really important Psalms scholar, Claus Westermann, reduced Gunkel's five to just two basic genres—praise and lament.[3] (Westermann identified thanksgiving as a form of praise.) Scholars have also renamed and recategorized some of the minor genres. However they are labeled, everyone agrees the task of genre analysis must be done and must be done well, which makes it extremely important for us to have some understanding of what the genres are and how they act. The list below reflects some of the more common genres as they are currently defined.

Praise Psalms: A praise psalm is … well, the best word for it is praise. The focus of their content is God. They acknowledge who God is believed to be (God's character) or celebrate some of God's big deeds accomplished in the past (e.g., creation, the exodus, other grand-scale redemptive stuff). Praise psalms are pretty obvious, especially since they often include the command, "Praise the LORD."[4] That's a bit of a giveaway. Because of their focus on the who and the what of God, we can think of praise psalms as representing the core theology of ancient Israel.

Lament Psalms: A lament psalm stands in contrast to a praise psalm. It's offered when the community's theological commitments don't seem to be working—when God is perceived as absent or avoidant, when enemies surround, sickness prevails, death is imminent, when anything that would occasion a plea for God to act on behalf of the psalmist occurs. Laments are also pretty easy to identify. If something has gone

---

[3] See Claus Westermann, *Praise and Lament in the Psalms*, trans. Keith R. Crim and Richard N. Soulen (Atlanta, GA: John Knox Press, 1981).

[4] The translation, "praise the LORD," in Hebrew is the phrase, *hallu yah*. The first word is an imperative verb, a command, meaning "you (pl.) praise." "Yah" is a shortened form of the divine name, *Yahweh*. This is where the word *hallelujah* comes from.

wrong and the psalmist is asking God to intervene, it's a lament. They can be offered by individuals or the community.

Thanksgiving Psalms: The thanksgiving psalms provide the end of the story that is begun in lament. A lament is a complaint and accompanying request for God to act, but by the end of the poem, you don't know if God will respond. The thanksgiving psalm provides an update in the form of a brief story. Here's an example: everything was off, I prayed to God, and God answered me. And then, in response, the psalmist offers a thanksgiving to God and to the wider worshipping community. Thanksgivings can also be offered by individuals or the community.

Royal Psalms and Torah Psalms: Royal psalms and torah psalms are two different categories. I have grouped them together because their identifications are both *content* (not form) *driven*. A royal psalm is about the king, and Torah psalms are about the Torah. Because of their clearly defined subject matter, they are both pretty easy to identify. If a psalmist seems overly concerned with one of these things, chances are, its genre will match their concern.

Pilgrimage Psalms: Pilgrimage psalms are believed to be written for Israelites journeying to the temple. The pray-ers are "on pilgrimage." These psalms describe the traveler's experience, culminating with their reaching the temple.

Mixed Genre: A mixed-genre psalm is a poem that combines elements of various genres. It's like a mash-up of a couple of different songs or (bad example) the now-heinous, then-popular "rap rock" of the early 2000s. Early genre analysts like Gunkel and Westermann thought mixed genre psalms were pretty common, but this is usually because the psalmists were not operating according to Gunkel's categories! Sometimes their work stumped him.

My appreciation of Gunkel's scholarly badassery notwithstanding, there is a recognizable level of intuition that we can apply in ascertaining a psalm's genre. Yes, they are old and foreign, but even an uninformed, modern reader could make good sense of some psalms fairly quickly. For fun, take a look at the following excerpts, and based on a simple assessment of the content and the overall tone of the poem, see if you can identify which one is the praise, lament, and thanksgiving.

> Why, O Lord, do you stand far off?
>> Why do you hide yourself in times of trouble?
> In arrogance the wicked persecute the poor—
>> let them be caught in the schemes they have devised.
>> (Ps 10:1–2)

> O Lord my God, I cried to you for help,
>> and you have healed me.
> O Lord, you brought up my soul from Sheol,
>> restored me to life from among those gone down to the Pit.
> Sing praises to the Lord, O you his faithful ones,
>> and give thanks to his holy name.
> For his anger is but for a moment;
>> his favor is for a lifetime.
> Weeping may linger for the night,
>> but joy comes with the morning.
>> (Ps 30:2–5)

> Rejoice in the Lord, O you righteous.
>> Praise befits the upright.
> Praise the Lord with the lyre;
>> make melody to him with the harp of ten strings.
> Sing to him a new song;
>> play skillfully on the strings, with loud shouts.
> For the word of the Lord is upright,
>> and all his work is done in faithfulness.

He loves righteousness and justice;
>> the earth is full of the steadfast love of the LORD.
>>> (Ps 33:1–5)

Easy, right?[5] The *content* of these psalms make the genre identification rather clear. There are distinct moods the psalms evoke or some key-words that almost give their genres away.

To be fair to Gunkel, genre analysis is not always this easy, especially when a psalmist seems to combine a few genres into one composition (the "mixed" genre, I mentioned above) or when it just isn't clear which genre is the best fit for a psalm.

At other times, a psalm is way too specific in what it's doing to fit one of the more general genre categories. In these cases, a new category might be created. For example, scholars identified Psalms 15 and 24 as "entrance liturgies" because the poems seem to include a liturgy for entering the temple. Some even proposed reading the two psalms as a script, a liturgical back-and-forth between the priest (or other official) and the potential worshipper. Viewed in this way, Psalm 15 can be read as follows:

Priest (to a potential worshipper at the gate):
O LORD, who may abide in your tent?
>> Who may dwell on your holy hill?

The Worshipper Seeking Admittance:
Those who walk blamelessly, and do what is right,
>> and speak the truth from their heart;
who do not slander with their tongue,
>> and do no evil to their friends,
nor take up a reproach against their neighbors;
>> in whose eyes the wicked are despised,
but who honor those who fear the LORD;

---

[5] They appeared in this order: lament, thanksgiving, praise.

who stand by their oath even to their hurt;
who do not lend money at interest,
and do not take a bribe against the innocent.

Priest:
Those who do these things shall never be moved.
Now get on in there, ya crazy kid.

OK, I added the last phrase, but the rest is in there. As you can see, the content drives the bus on how the psalm is believed to function. Indeed, when it is broken up in this way, with the speaker labels affixed, you can see what the scholars are saying. It's plausible that the psalm could have been used as a liturgical script.

Not everyone agrees, of course, because the category was based entirely on speculation. There are no instructions and no speaker designations in the psalm specifying how it was supposed to be used. Scholars are just guessing. And even though it seems like a good guess, there are other, equally viable options for these psalms beyond "entrance liturgy."[6]

The "entrance liturgy" example is an important one because it demonstrates the limitations of genre identification. (1) Sometimes scholars are guessing. It's an informed guess to be sure, but at the end of the day, it's impossible to know what was going on in a psalm's ancient context. (2) If an interpreter lands on a specific genre, they are pretty locked in to how they think the psalm was used in Israel's past (like, as a dialogue between a priestly figure and a potential worshipper), and maybe, along with that, how they view the psalm's use now (e.g., maybe the proposed entrance liturgy becomes a call to worship). As a result, they might be blinded to other potential uses. And (3) some folks would respond, "Stop guessing! Just focus on what the psalm

---

[6] See John T. Willis, "Ethics in a Cultic Setting," in *Essays in Old Testament Ethics*, ed. James L. Crenshaw and John T. Willis (New York: KTAV Publishing House, 1974), 145-69 (154).

says." John T. Willis, for example, convincingly argues that when we read Psalms 15 and 24 as "entrance liturgies," we tend to overlook their ethical instruction.

What Worship Music, Hallmark Christmas Movies, and Psalms' Genres Have in Common

Part of the genius of Gunkel's work was moving the task of genre analysis beyond the content of the psalm to also include an assessment of its *formal literary characteristics*. By formal literary characteristics I mean how a poem moves, how it is ordered or structured, what formal elements are included, and when or in what order they appear in the poem. (Side note: this is why Gunkel's interpretive method was called "*form* criticism." It focused on the *form* of a genre, and how, say, a praise psalm or a lament psalm was structured.)

Here's an example. Gunkel claimed a thanksgiving psalm always includes a "narrative retelling of the one giving thanks." By narrative retelling, Gunkel meant the psalmist's story or testimony, which he says, is "never lacking" in a thanksgiving psalm.[7] In the excerpt of a thanksgiving psalm I provided above, the psalmist writes: I cried to you [Yahweh] and you healed me, you brought me up from Sheol, you restored me to life. The story is admittedly terse. It's not what we might typically define as a "narrative," but it does recount what happened in the psalmist's life—I cried to you, you healed me, you restored my life. This story/experience occasions the offering of thanksgiving. According to Brueggemann and Bellinger, a good way to summarize the "plot" of the psalmists' stories and its result is: *need–petition–rescue–thanks*.[8] If some variant of this progression isn't present, it's not a thanksgiving psalm.

---

[7] Gunkel, *Introduction to Psalms*, 201.
[8] See Walter Brueggemann and William H. Bellinger, Jr., *Psalms* (New Cambridge Bible Commentary; New York: Cambridge University Press, 2014), 151.

More often, it's not just the fact *that* a formal element, like a story, appears ... it's *where* it appears or in what *order* it appears. Think about music for a second. Musical genres have an expected order or structure to them. For example, you can usually tell when a guitar solo or a dramatic key change or a "breakdown" is coming in a song. If you know the genre well, it's predictable, almost formulaic. Everything in the song leads to these dramatic moments. For my church folks, contemporary Christian worship music provides an easy example of an expected song structure: Intro (featuring a guitar with dotted eighth notes and a reverb pedal), Verse 1, Verse 2, (soft, acoustic) Chorus, (bring everything back in for) Verse 3, (a big) Chorus, (an even bigger) Chorus, A BIG HUGE EMOTIONAL BRIDGE, (another big) Chorus, (a soft) Chorus, Outro.

If you're more of a film buff, movie genres provide another example of stereotyped structure. There are plot progressions we expect from certain movie genres, whether they are rom-coms or scary movies or a feel-good, Disney sports biopic. They all usually follow a similar pattern. Hallmark Christmas movies provide an *extreme* example of expected structure. If you've seen one of these movies, you've seen them all, because they have the same general plot. Every. Single. Time. And it's wonderful. If, by the end, there's no dramatic kiss shared between an unlikely/totally-expected couple at a community-wide Christmas extravaganza in a quaint country town with twinkly lights, then, it's not a Hallmark Christmas movie.

Now apply the idea of an assumed structure in music and movies to the psalms' genres. According to Gunkel, each genre has its own expected movement, its own predictable form or structure. Like an anthemic church-y worship song or a Hallmark Christmas movie, there are certain formal literary characteristics that are operative in a given genre.

The proposed form of a praise psalm, for example, begins with an initial "call to praise," then moves to the "reasons/motivations for praise." It might end here or it might conclude with another "call to praise." There is some flexibility in the form. Psalm 117 provides a really straightforward example:

Call to Praise
> Praise the LORD, all you nations!
>> Extol him, all you peoples! (v. 1)

Reasons/Motivations
> For great is his steadfast love toward us,
>> and the faithfulness of the LORD endures forever. (v. 2ab)

Final Call to Praise
> Praise the LORD! (v. 2c)

That's it. That's the whole psalm. And it checks all of the boxes. It moves seamlessly from the initial call to praise to the reasons for praise to a final call to praise. It has all the formal literary characteristics of a praise psalm.

Gunkel's assessment of a psalm's genre by appealing to its form and content has been incredibly helpful for readers of Psalms. It moved them beyond unanswerable historical questions like who wrote it, when was it written, and why was it written. It also demonstrates that the psalmists don't usually "go rogue." (They don't always obey Gunkel, but that's more of an "us"-problem.) There is no free verse or spoken word or slam poetry in Psalms. There are rules. There are patterns. As a result, there are very few poems in the collection of which you would say, "This one doesn't fit at all!" And that's because there was a set of forms that worked to constrain the psalmists and their poetic endeavors.[9]

---

[9] To be fair, this is all a little subjective. When Gunkel says a genre has an anticipated structure, *he was the one anticipating the structure!* Still, he was right to call attention to the recurring patterns that the psalms' genres seem to follow, and his work helped to set the standard to which later scholars have introduced important clarifications and advancements.

Seeking a *Sitz im Leben* ... As One Does

Gunkel's other major contribution to Psalms studies was his attempted recovery of a psalm's social setting (its *Sitz im Leben*, "setting in life"). According to Gunkel, this was much more important and much more attainable than trying to reconstruct all of those unanswerable historical inquiries that dominated Psalms scholarship in his day. He proposed asking about the setting in which a psalm was *used*. The inquiry was more about *how* or *in what way* a psalm functioned than anything else.

While Gunkel's view on the social setting(s) of the psalms developed over the course of his career, he eventually claimed that the overwhelming majority of psalms originated for use in communal worship. They were *liturgical*.

Think again of the proposed genre of the "entrance liturgy." People used the form of the psalm to conceptualize its use *in worship*. It was deemed to be a script for a priest at the gate and a worshipper wishing to gain admittance into the temple complex. That was its literary form, but also, its purported "social setting."

Sometimes a psalm's content can help elucidate how it may have been used. For example, at the conclusion of Psalm 116, the psalmist writes,

> I will offer to you a thanksgiving sacrifice
> > and call on the name of the LORD.
> I will pay my vows to the LORD
> > in the presence of all his people,
> in the courts of the house of the LORD,
> > in your midst, O Jerusalem.
> Praise the LORD! (vv. 17–19)

Because of what the psalm says about sacrifice, the psalm was believed to function in ancient Israelite worship as the *means* of sacrifice. The thanksgiving was to be voiced in public as an offering to God and to fulfill a vow made by the pray-er when they lamented. They pledged to God that if they were delivered, they would "sacrifice." The proposal is, the psalm functioned as a thank-offering.

My point is not to affirm the above interpretive conclusions. (It's impossible to know.) Rather, I want to point out how people in Gunkel's time were approaching Psalms—they would look for clues in a psalm regarding its use in worship and then hypothesize a social setting. Some people took this way too far. One of Gunkel's students famously hypothesized one specific festival as the context for Psalms.[10] His proposal, while novel, was eventually rejected due to its speculative nature. It's difficult to move beyond the broad claim that psalms were used in worship. How and when and why is more difficult to say.

Where All of this Led

When Gunkel emerged onto the scene, he was working in a field that was dominated by historical-critical concerns. And when your focus is Psalms studies, it's difficult to make any headway on those sorts of concerns for the reasons we have already outlined. Gunkel helped to move interpreters beyond the impasse by turning his attention to genre and social setting. A by-product of this is, once you get past the need to place individual psalms in a specific historical and/or religious context, you can begin to celebrate the psalms for what they are, namely, beautiful pieces of meaningful and theologically significant literary art. Gunkel's work paved the way for viewing the psalms in this way (well, once people stopped trying to nail down a specific festival in which Psalms may have been used). That was the next big move in Psalms

---

[10] His name was Sigmund Mowinckel. If you read any other introduction to Psalms, you will definitely get more information on Mowinckel and the "Enthronement of Yahweh." But here's the thing, nobody thinks he was right. So I don't feel too bad about relegating him to the footnotes.

studies, and it was part of a much larger move in biblical scholarship called the literary turn. Interpreters focused *on the text as we have it.*

In Psalms scholarship, that meant people were concentrating on individual poems (or single genres), which is still how most people tend to read Psalms today. It's typically approached as a collection of individual poems, randomly (or haphazardly) grouped together. And so, readers take it one psalm at a time and focus their interpretive energy on that one psalm's artistry and message, its form and its content. We don't tend to think of Psalms as a *book*. We treat it, instead, like a Spotify recommended playlist on shuffle. We'll listen to whatever song comes up without thinking of what's next.

We'll come back to the idea of the structure of Psalms as a whole in Chapter Seven, but first, I need to tell you something important about reading individual psalms and where the literary turn took us.

CHAPTER SIX

The Psalms are Poetic

Beyond properly identifying its genre, if we are to understand what in the world is going on in a given psalm, we will need to attend to its poetry. That means we need to know something about biblical Hebrew poetry. Note the modifiers I use here. It's not just poetry, it's *biblical Hebrew* poetry. That's important. Many modern readers come to the Bible with preconceptions about poetry. I'd guess most of these preconceptions come from exposure to poets like Emily Dickinson and Langston Hughes and, my personal favorite, E.E. Cummings, in high-school English classes. There, we learned poetry is about rhyme and meter and, at least in the case of the Japanese haiku, syllable count.

The good news is this knowledge isn't *totally* useless for reading the Psalms—although I should say, biblical Hebrew poetry doesn't typically rhyme. And despite much effort, no one has been able to crack the code regarding its meter. It's not as regimented as, say, Shakespeare's use of iambic pentameter.[1] Also, while some folks like to count syllables, that, too, is quite subjective (since there are so many unanswered questions about Hebrew pronunciation). Many of

---

[1] In their introductory work on Hebrew poetry, David L. Petersen and Kent Harold Richards conclude, "[I]t seems appropriate to delete meter as a category for understanding biblical Hebrew poetry." See David L. Petersen and Kent Harold Richards, *Interpreting Hebrew Poetry* (Guides to Biblical Scholarship; Minneapolis: Fortress Press, 1992), 42.

our English-class-influenced expectations have not yielded significant or predictable results when applied to biblical Hebrew poetry.

Still, there are *some* similarities between English poetry and Psalms. One is pretty obvious—just like the poetry in your freshmen-level Norton Anthology, biblical Hebrew poetry is very economical with word usage. Poets convey powerful images in very few words. There is no "It was a dark and stormy night…" in poetry. It's terse. As a result, poetry looks distinct on the page. Just think about how much white space appears when you are reading poetic texts. For fun, flip through your copy of the Bible and observe the margins. It's clear when the editors *think* they are dealing with a poetic text because the formatting changes.[2]

Poetry's economy with words encourages a slow and rhythmic reading. This is why some scholars prefer to talk about the "rhythm" of biblical Hebrew poetry as a defining characteristic instead of a more technical (and regimented) term like meter. Rhythm is defined by Terry Brogan as "a cadence, a contour, a figure of periodicity, any sequence perceptible as a distinct pattern capable of repetition and variation."[3] Even a novice can feel it. There is a rhythm, a flow, a "bob your head and rock back-and-forth" sort of movement to biblical Hebrew poetry.

The standard division of a poetic line encourages its rhythmic feel. And here, we start to venture into some of the unique qualities that make biblical Hebrew poetry … *biblical Hebrew* poetry. Take Psalm 13:1 as an example. It reads,

> How long, O Lord? Will you forget me forever?
> How long will you hide your face from me?

---

[2] Deciding how to format the page is an editor's/translator's choice, especially in an otherwise predominantly narrative work. Check out Genesis, for example, and notice when the formatting switches from prose to poetry. There is nothing in the Hebrew text that demands this. It's a choice made by the translator.

[3] Cited in Petersen and Richards, *Interpreting Hebrew Poetry*, 37.

Real quick, let's talk terminology. This entire construction can be referred to as a verse, a sentence, or a line—I'll use the term "line"—and each component part, each "How long …," can be called a verset, a half-verse, a line (yes, I know I already said that), a stich, a hemistich, a colon, or simply, A and B. For ease, I'll label the individual parts of a line as A and B (and if needed, C). If we need to speak more generally about the individual parts of a line, I'll call each one a colon (plural: cola).

The poetic structuring device of hinged half-lines in biblical Hebrew poetry is a really important building block of its poetic system—and that building block is called parallelism.

Parallelism

We can think of parallelism in this way: the two (or three) component parts (cola) of a poetic line are parallel in some way. They are related or connected. They are tied together. Spatially, it can represented in this way:

_____A_____ / _____B_____ //

Or, if we are dealing with a "tri-colon" (a line with three cola):

_____A_____ / _____B_____ / _____C_____ //

The break in the line, visually represented by a single slash (/), indicates a pause between A and B (and C). It's rhythmic. But, more importantly, the pause between cola indicates a relationship of some sort. In contrast, the double slash (//) at the end of the line indicates a full stop. Biblical Hebrew poetry does not consist in "two complete, utterly independent, yet in some respects parallel utterances."[4] In other words, there are no single lines constructed as follows:

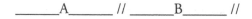

_____A_____ // _____B_____ //

The pause between cola is where the line's meaning resides, and it's up to the interpreter to correctly deduce how the two are related.

Let's look again at Psalm 13:1.

[A] How long, O LORD? Will you forget me forever? /
   [B] How long will you hide your face from me? //

At first glance, there does not appear to be a whole lot of difference between the sense of colon A and colon B. In fact, it might seem as if the poet is saying the same thing twice. Both cola voice the fact that Yahweh is not present. Yahweh has forgotten the psalmist in A. Yahweh is hiding from the psalmist in B. The psalmist feels alone and isolated. They want to know how long this will continue.

At this point in discussions on parallelism, Robert Lowth's massively influential work, *De sacra poesi Hebraeorum (The Sacred Poetry of the Hebrews)*, is usually cited. You know a book is serious … and old … when the title is in Latin. And this is no exception. It was written in 1753, and it remains a mandatory conversation partner in discussions of biblical Hebrew poetry. That's because it was here that Lowth introduced the concept of parallelism. He famously proposed three types: synonymous, antithetical, and synthetic parallelism.

According to Lowth's system, Psalm 13:1 would be an example of synonymous parallelism. The two cola appear to say the same thing: Yahweh is nowhere to be found. (There is more to it, as I will explain below, but let me define Lowth's other two categories first.)

---

[4] James L. Kugel, *The Idea of Biblical Poetry: Parallelism and Its History* (Baltimore, MD: The Johns Hopkins University Press, 1981), 52.

The next type of parallelism is called antithetical parallelism. In this construction, A and B are antonyms. In a way, this is a variant of synonymous parallelism, because linking two opposites is a different way of "saying the same thing." Here's an example:

> [A] For the LORD watches over the way of *the righteous*, /
> [B] but the way of *the wicked* will perish. //
> (Ps 1:6)

The third type of parallelism proposed by Lowth is called synthetic parallelism. This designation functions as a catchall for all the other potential relationships between cola (i.e., not synonymous or antithetical). The most one can say is, in synthetic parallelism, B "finishes" the thought of A somehow.

> [A] From the rising of the sun to its setting, /
> [B] the name of the LORD is to be praised. //
> (Ps 113:3)

The problem with synthetic parallelism is how broad it is. Other than the fact that the line isn't synonymous or antithetical parallelism, there are few discernible similarities between the proposed "examples" of this phenomena. Rolf A. Jacobson and Karl N. Jacobson conclude, "if you have a catchall category such as 'synthetic parallelism' to fit in everything that does not fit into your other categories, maybe there is a problem with your categories."[5]

For years (centuries, in fact!), Lowth's categories ruled the day. More recently, however, they have been called into question.

---

[5] Jacobson and Jacobson, *Invitation to the Psalms*, 12.

A is So … and What's More, B.

About 40 years ago, two Jewish scholars said (I'm paraphrasing), "Synonymous parallelism doesn't make any sense. B sounds similar to A, but it's not the same. It can't be. It's the same with antithetical parallelism. A poet wouldn't merely repeat themselves. B is a furthering … a heightening … a movement beyond A." The first to make this case, James Kugel, suggests we should think of the relationship between cola in this way: "A is so and what's more, B."[6] B says *something more* than A. It moves the reader *beyond* A.

Let's look one more time at Psalm 13:1.

[A] How long, O Lord? Will you forget me forever? /
[B] How long will you hide your face from me? //

When you think about it, there are some pretty big differences between Yahweh's forgetting (in A) and Yahweh's hiding (in B). The first verb is passive—you don't set out to forget, it just happens. But the second verb is active—you actually have to hide from someone. It takes effort. It takes intention. Another difference is, the first verb is sort of abstract—forgetting someone depersonalizes it a bit. They just slip your mind. But the second verb, Yahweh's hiding, is much more personal. Yahweh is hiding Yahweh's face *from the psalmist*. Seemingly, in B, the writer is emphasizing just how far the situation has gone. Not only has Yahweh forgotten—Yahweh sees and acknowledges the psalmist's suffering, and is choosing not to engage. Yahweh is choosing to actively hide from the suppliant.

A is so (Yahweh forgets) … and what's more, B (Yahweh hides Yahweh's face from the psalmist). The second colon is not restating the same thing. It's moving beyond it.

A few years later in *The Art of Biblical Poetry*, Robert Alter made a similar case. He talks about the "dynamic movement" in poetic par-

---

[6] See Kugel, *The Idea of Biblical Poetry*, 1–58.

allelism.[7] Like Kugel, he contends there is no such thing as a true synonym. Alter claims you can't pick different words from a thesaurus to create the equation A=B. Words might overlap in meaning, but what they communicate and the way they communicate is entirely unique. Alter writes, "Six inches and half a foot may be exact quantitative equivalents, but they are not true synonyms...."[8] The descriptions have a different feel. They conjure up different images in the mind of the reader. Depending on what is being described, "half a foot," communicates something much more extravagantly (and aggressively) than "six inches."

Here's another example of the furthering aspect at work in parallelism: Psalm 3:7b. After calling on God to "rise up" and "deliver me" (which is also a dynamic movement from the general to the specific) in 3:7a, the psalmist writes,

[A] For you strike all my enemies on the cheek; /
    [B] you break the teeth of the wicked. //

If we are reading this line through the lens of synonymous parallelism, "strike the cheek" and "break the teeth" are quickly aligned. They might even be viewed as two ways of saying the same thing. But upon further reflection, the sentiment of B is much more pointed, much more intense. The line moves from striking or hitting on the cheek to breaking or smashing teeth. There's a movement from no information on the effect (striking the cheek) to stating the result (breaking teeth), from the external (cheek) to the internal (in the mouth), from the general to the specific. A is so ... and what's more, B.

One more example: Psalm 135:5.

[A] For I know that the LORD is great; /
    [B] our Lord is above all gods. //

---

[7] Robert Alter, *The Art of Biblical Poetry* (New York: Basic Books, 1985), 10.
[8] Alter, *The Art of Biblical Poetry*, 13.

In A, the psalmist states that Yahweh is great. In B, the psalmist advances the statement by offering a comparison of just *how* great Yahweh is—Yahweh is above or better than all other, rival gods (more on that in the Chapter Eight). The psalmist furthers the point.

A is so … and what's more, B.

Is That It? Is That All We Need to Know?

Parallelism is by no means the only thing that characterizes biblical Hebrew poetry, but it is really important. If we grasp this concept, we are well on our way to interpreting poetic texts in the Hebrew Bible.

Reading poetry in any language, however, demands that one also interpret other expected literary conventions well. This includes noting the use of common word pairs (e.g., righteous/wicked, day/night, heaven/earth) and the repetition of words/concepts in poetic lines, and any distinctive, structural patterns, such as the use of repeated refrains (e.g., "the steadfast love of the Lord endures forever" after each line, as in Psalm 136) or specific word patterns. A "chiasm," also known as a reverse pattern, is a good example of the latter.

There are many different types of chiasms. Here's one:

[A] If I forget you, O Jerusalem,
   [B] let my right hand wither!
   [B] Let my tongue cling to the roof of my mouth,
[A] if I do not remember you,

(Ps 137:5–6a)

The repetition in a chiasm can be based on a number of things—words, ideas/themes, grammatical or syntactic elements. Also, a chiasm can be found in a single line, a few lines, or over the course of an entire poem. There is a lot of diversity. In the above example, the chiasm extends over a couple of lines: the A cola are related to each other thematically and syntactically, as are the B cola.

Some people love to mine for chiasms.[9] And if you are dead set on finding one, you probably will, so be careful.

An *alphabetic acrostic* is another example of a structural device. This is when a poet begins the first word of the first line (or colon) of a poem with a word that starts with the first letter of the alphabet, then the first word of the second line (or colon) with a word that starts with the second letter of the alphabet, and so on down the line. It's the equivalent of writing a poem in English where the first letter of each line or poetic phrase moves sequentially through the English alphabet from A to Z.

Psalm 119 is an alphabetic acrostic on steroids, moving sequentially in groups of eight poetic lines *per letter*. It begins its first line with a word that starts with the first letter of the Hebrew alphabet, *aleph*. Then it repeats this pattern for the next seven lines—all of which begin with an "*aleph* word." The first word of the next eight lines begin with the next letter of the Hebrew alphabet, *bet*. The poet then goes letter by letter, in sequence. The artistry is impressive, and the effect even more so. For a poem about how great the *torah* is, this poetic structuring device signals a completeness or exhaustiveness—an annoying amount, really—of praise for God's instruction. (*Torah* is broader than "law"; it can mean teaching, instruction, and law.)

Reading poetry also demands close attention to the author's use of imagery. Metaphor and simile are prominent in biblical Hebrew poetry—examples of both abound in Psalms. As we've already discussed, the distance from our cultural context to the one depicted in the text ups the level of interpretive difficulty. We will see how this plays out more fully in the second section of this book.

If you would like to dive into the minutia of poetic language, refer to my recommended resources at the back of this book. Rather than spending time defining terms like anaphora, alliteration, enjambment,

---

[9] I remember a seminary professor talking about a colleague they referred to as "Captain Chiasm"—which is, I'm sure, a devastating attack in the world of biblical scholarship.

and *inclusio*, I think we would be better served by reading some psalms and seeing how various poetic techniques work in actual practice. But before we do, there is one more introductory issue we need to address: how to read Psalms *as a book*.

CHAPTER SEVEN

Reading Psalms as a Mixtape

Gunkel's form-critical method and the advancements applied to it in the so-called "literary turn" kept readers' attention on one psalm at a time. The interpretive focus on a single psalm's genre, social setting, and literary artistry would be equivalent to putting on your headphones, hitting repeat on your favorite song, and trancing out. All of that attention helps the listener to become an expert on the song's chord progression, lyrics, instrumentation, hook, feeling, and structure. But it also means the song's larger setting—on, say, an album, EP, or playlist—is neglected.

For years, that's where Psalms scholarship lived, at the level of intense, focused attention to individual psalms. And then, a few decades ago, people began asking a much larger question that was also influenced by literary criticism ...

What Do You Do with Psalms as a Collection?

I've been getting some mileage out of the analogy of Psalms as an expertly crafted Spotify playlist, but let's think about the direct precursor to a playlist for some added depth: mixtapes or mix CDs. When I was in high school and college, it was the age of Napster, huge desktop computers, and burning CDs. So like many music-loving American youths at the time, I made a lot of mix CDs, and not a few were my attempts to organize the most romantic, most moving, most objectively beautiful collection of "emo" music ever compiled in order to win the affections of a crush. Every song on these mixes had its place, and I, as the architect of this unique collection, would spend hours thinking about the connections between the songs—how they moved, the story they told, the emotions they might elicit, the fade out from one song into the intro of the next. Like the words printed on a Hallmark card, these songs, in *this particular order*, would speak for me (as would the "Sharpie art" used to decorate a plain white CD-R).

For all of the reasons I outlined in Chapter One—the signs in the text that point to Psalms' development, its intentionally placed introduction and conclusion, the editorial division of Psalms into five "books"—some scholars began to think about the shape of Psalms *as a whole*. Are its 150 poems related? Are they in some sort of order? Did the compiler/editor of the collection have an intention beyond simply adding more good poems when they became available? Is the book meant to be seen as something other than a random compilation of "singles"? Does it tell a story? Is it … a mix CD made with love and decorated with a Sharpie?

Finding Order in the Life of Faith

For one viewpoint, let's consider the proposal of noted Bible scholar, Walter Brueggemann. Brueggemann has written a ton of stuff on Psalms. You can think of him, in terms of influence, as a current-day "Hermann Gunkel" in the world of Psalms studies. In one of his early essays on Psalms, Brueggemann addressed the issue of genre diversity.[1] He noted how reading Psalms from beginning to end seems to move

---

[1] Walter Brueggemann, "Psalms and the Life of Faith: A Suggested Typology of Function," *Journal for the Study of the Old Testament* 17 (1980): 3–32.

the reader indiscriminately and sometimes abruptly from one genre to the next. In view of the book's unpredictable amalgamation of genres, Brueggemann suggested the imposition of three thematic categories to help make sense of the book's structure. He titled them: psalms of orientation, psalms of disorientation, and psalms of new orientation. For Brueggemann, these categories, and their unpredictable appearance in Psalms, are emblematic of the life of faith.

Psalms of Orientation. These psalms present ancient Israel's "core theology." It's like the poetic version of Israel's "statement of faith." In these contributions, God is present. God listens. God responds. Things are as they should be. The world works. The good get good and the bad get judged. As a result, the psalmists writing psalms of orientation are very grounded, very settled, very content even, because the world (apparently) is moving according to plan. That's why most of the psalms of orientation are praise psalms. This category also includes Torah psalms and royal psalms—whatever describes the world as it "should be."

Psalms of Disorientation. Life isn't always as it "should be." It doesn't always work. It doesn't always make sense. In fact, a lot of times, it feels as though God is not present, not listening, not responding. The psalms of disorientation lean into this reality and offer readers a forceful and much-needed "counter-testimony" to the psalms of orientation. These two categories, then, are in dialogue. (Brueggemann often uses language of testimony and counter-testimony to describe Psalms and, more generally, the Hebrew Bible.[2] He is also fond of thinking of things in terms of dialogue.)

The lament psalms serve as the primary witness to the psalmists' experience of life *not working*—of enemies surrounding, death threatening, sickness invading, and God seeming not to care—and there are a lot of them. If you are reading the book in order, it doesn't take too

---

[2] See Walter Brueggemann, *Theology of the Old Testament: Testimony, Dispute, Advocacy* (Minneapolis: Fortress Press, 1997).

long to find one. In fact, the first, Psalm 3, sits right next to two psalms of orientation (Psalms 1 and 2). This is weird because Psalm 1 has said that if you obey the Torah, if you meditate on it, if you order your life around it, you'll be prosperous. But apparently, that's not real life. Psalm 3 begins,

> "O LORD, how many are my foes!
>   Many are rising against me;
> many are saying to me,
>   'There is no help for you in God.'" (vv. 1–2)

Psalms of disorientation, like Psalm 3, challenge the truthfulness of what Israel believes, and they do so by offering an honest assessment (dialogue) of what the psalmist is experiencing.

Psalms of New Orientation. The things represented in the psalms of disorientation often resolve. Chaos is ordered. The threat of enemies or sickness or death is removed. God responds ... eventually. The book of Psalms includes compositions reflecting these situations too, most notably, the psalms of thanksgiving. These psalms provide a witness of what's on the other side of lament; they tell you how the petition/protest/plea was resolved. Remember, as a genre, the thanksgiving psalms include a narrative moving from the psalmist's need, to their prayer to Yahweh for deliverance (these first two elements feature in the lament psalms too), and then their experience of divine deliverance.

Orientation—disorientation—new orientation. For Brueggemann, these categories provide a thematic pattern and a sense of coherence for the whole book. Readers, he argues, experience this pattern throughout their lives, from their own seasons of orientation to the unsettled dialogue offered in seasons of disorientation to the resolution offered in those moments when new orientation occurs. And this pattern doesn't happen once. It keeps happening, and each time through the cycle changes us, forms us, shapes us.[3]

Brueggemann is definitely not reading Psalms as an intentionally, editorially shaped collection from start to finish, at least not beyond the now standard scholarly acknowledgment of the collection's introduction and conclusion. But I have found Brueggemann's structural suggestion to be really helpful because what he offers is a presentation of Psalms in dialogue. This conversational outlook helps us move beyond hitting repeat on individual psalms to thinking about how the different genres relate to one another. Brueggemann seems to be saying, "Look at how diverse the psalms are. There's not much rhyme or reason to when any one genre shows up. Seems like life doesn't it? Some psalms offer a core testimony—they orient us. And then others complain, 'The core testimony isn't working. It's broken. I have enemies all around me. God doesn't care.' And then others add another layer by countering, 'I know what you mean, but stick with it. It *does* work. It did for me, and I bet it can for you too.'" It's a very pastoral approach.

Reading Psalms as a Mixtape

Some scholars go further in their attempts to identify a reason and rationality behind the ordering of Psalms' poems. They argue that the book's compilers arranged (and rearranged) the individual psalms from start to finish. In contrast to Brueggemann's suggestion, this is not seen as an *imposed* structure on the book ... it's an *intended* structure created by Psalms' editors. The collection, in other words, is viewed as a mixtape created with tender loving care for a high-school crush. Every psalm has its place. Every psalm makes sense in light of the larger collection. They all move together. They tell a story when read in sequence.

---

[3] See also John Goldingay, "The Dynamic Cycle of Praise and Prayer," *Journal for the Study of the Old Testament* 20 (1985): 85–90.

And as a result, when you look at one psalm, you need to think about the surrounding psalms too or you might miss something.

Clearly, when you are trying to argue for the editorial intention of a book like Psalms, it's difficult to prove. It's too subjective. It's too speculative. That's one knock against this approach, and it's definitely worth a listen. If you set out to demonstrate thematic or linguistic links between psalms, which use standardized language and are already fairly similar, you can probably find what you are looking for. But, again, when you factor in all of the "evidence" of redaction we introduced in Chapter One, it's possible to make a case for Psalms' intentional and thoroughgoing editorial activity.

Rather than zooming in and dissecting the relationship between random psalms that exist side-by-side in Psalms (those studies are out there, but in my opinion, they fall prey to some of the subjectivity I mentioned above), I will offer a deeper look at the structure of the five books of Psalms. Over the last few decades, interpreters have proposed reading these books as distinct "chapters" or "episodes" in a unified narrative retelling of Israel's story from the time of David to the exile, and the results are interesting to say the least. It goes like this:

Book 1 (Psalms 1–41) is all about David. Once we get past Psalms 1 and 2, every composition in this book is a *ledawid* psalm. Regardless of how we interpret that phrase, there is an undeniable focus in Book 1 on the person of David. Some readers see the high prevalence of "David psalms" as a sign of intentional editing, as if we are supposed to read Book 1 through a David lens.

From the standpoint of genre, Book 1 favors lament, but it also includes a good number of praise psalms. The diversity of content that is present allows readers to see Book 1 as a collection of prayers that *could have been used* during the reign of David in situations ranging from moments of praise to moments of perceived abandonment and struggle. According to Nancy L. deClaissé-Walford, the reader is "drawn into the world of the monarchy of ancient Israel."

Book 2 (Psalms 42–72) continues the focus on David and his story. Again, this is largely based on the editorial notes in the psalm titles, as more than half of the compositions are *ledawid* psalms. Interestingly, the penultimate psalm of Book 2, Psalm 71, is the only composition in the book without a title. The psalmist is depicted as an old man, near the end of life. It's curious that the psalm isn't specifically linked with David, but it could easily symbolize an unnamed, old David reflecting on his life. This observation is heightened when one considers the editorial note at the end of Book 2, where, after the editor's doxological conclusion, we read, "The prayers of David son of Jesse are ended" (72:20).

The proposed "story" of Psalms in Books 1 and 2, then, is thought to set up a movement beyond David. By the end of Book 2, his prayers have ended and his "kingship" is over.[4] To make the case even stronger, the title of Psalm 72, the last psalm in Book 2, identifies it as a "psalm of/to/for/on behalf of/inspired by/concerning/about/dedicated to/belonging to *Solomon*." It's a transitional psalm. In the story being told in Psalms, David's kingship is over, and Solomon's begins. The story doesn't spend much time lingering here, for in Book 3, the editor will take us beyond Solomon to the time of the divided monarchy (more on that below) and eventually to Babylonian exile in the 6th century BCE.

Book 3 (Psalms 73–89) is the shortest collection in Psalms. It includes only 17 psalms. The majority of them are community hymns and community laments, which is odd when compared with the rest of the collection. The focus in Book 3 is not on "I" but "we." According to the proponents of reading Psalms as a mixtape, this shift makes perfect sense. In the story being told, the Northern Kingdom of Israel

---

[4] Well, in the proposed story of Psalms, it is over. Remember, more *ledawid* psalms appear in Books 3–5, which is an oddity of the "Psalms as intentionally shaped" theory. Admittedly, David plays a less significant role in Books 3–5, but he still appears.

has fallen. This is clarified in a psalm like Psalm 78, typically dubbed a "narrative psalm" or "historical psalm." It retells the story of Israel, of its recalcitrance and rebellion, and of God's judgment. The latter is vividly and climactically portrayed in Israel's defeat by Assyrian forces in 722 BCE. Even though the event is not specifically mentioned in Psalm 78, its "story" appeals to the Northern Kingdom's defeat. The psalmist writes,

> [God] abandoned his dwelling at Shiloh,
>   the tent where he dwelt among mortals,
> and delivered his power to captivity,
>   his glory to the hand of the foe. (vv. 60–61)

And

> He rejected the tent of Joseph,
>   he did not choose the tribe of Ephraim;
> but he chose the tribe of Judah,
>   Mount Zion, which he loves. (vv. 67–68)

According to the biblical narrative, the monarchy was divided into two separate kingdoms after Solomon's reign. Each kingdom had their own king, capital, center of worship, and political alliances. "Israel" consisted of the 10 northern tribes, one of which was Ephraim. (In fact, the Northern Kingdom of Israel is often identified as Ephraim in the Hebrew Bible.) Its center of worship was in Shiloh. We see both of these identifiers in Psalm 78: God "abandoned his dwelling *at Shiloh*" and "did not choose *the tribe of Ephraim*." The kingdom of Israel, in other words, had been rejected, and was given over to punishment.

The other political entity resulting from the divided kingdom, Judah, consisted of the two southernmost tribes of Judah and Benjamin. It fell too, about 150 years after Israel. Nancy L. deClaissé-Walford and Gerald H. Wilson[5] call attention to the depiction of the Southern Kingdom's monumental defeat in Book 3. A perfectly placed royal psalm at the end of the book describes the event in no uncertain terms.

The first part of Psalm 89 appeals to the promises given to David ... and then, by the end, laments his/their rejection.

> You [God] said, "I have made a covenant with my chosen one,
>   I have sworn to my servant David:
> 'I will establish your descendants forever,
>   and build your throne for all generations.'"(vv. 3–4)

> "Once and for all I [God] have sworn by my holiness;
>   I will not lie to David.
> His line shall continue forever,
>   and his throne endure before me like the sun.
> It shall be established forever like the moon,
>   an enduring witness in the skies." (vv. 35–37)

> But now you [God] have spurned and rejected him [David];
>   you are full of wrath against your anointed.
> You have renounced the covenant with your servant;
>   you have defiled his crown in the dust. (vv. 38–39)

---

[5] Gerald H. Wilson is actually *the person* who put a storied approach to Psalms on the map. If you're curious about his argument, check out the essay, "The Structure of the Psalter" in *Interpreting the Psalms: Issues and Approaches*, David Firth and Philip S. Johnston, eds. (Downers Grove, IL: IVP Academic, 2005), 229–46. Before his untimely death, Wilson also finished the first volume of a planned two-volume commentary on Psalms in the *New International Version Application Commentary* series. This work assumes the editorial shaping of the Psalms. It is both very helpful and very pastoral. See Gerald H. Wilson, *Psalms Volume 1* (NIVAC; Grand Rapids, MI: Zondervan, 2002).

It's not explicitly stated, but it's clear. The psalmist is describing the fall of Judah to Babylon. The people have no king, no temple, and little hope. The psalm concludes with an unanswered lament.

> Lord, where is your steadfast love of old,
>> which by your faithfulness you swore to David?
> Remember, O Lord, how your servant is taunted;
>> how I bear in my bosom the insults of the peoples,
> with which your enemies taunt, O Lord,
>> with which they taunted the footsteps of your anointed.
>
> (vv. 49–51)

I want you to catch this … the psalmist is unloading some *serious* language *against Yahweh*. In fact, "unanswered lament" is probably too tame of a term for what is happening here. The psalmist is basically calling the God of the covenant a big, fat liar. All of the promises outlined in the first half of the poem provide a dramatic setup for this stunning conclusion by the psalmist—God's word has not been kept. David/Judah has been rejected. The people are in exile. And God doesn't care.

Some suggest that Books 1–3 represent an early, exilic version of Psalms, with Books 4 and 5 ("the rest of the story," as it were) being added later. Maybe. It's impossible to know. But if Psalms is shaped to tell a story, by the end of Book 3 the narrative has covered David's kingship, the division of the kingdom, and the eventual defeat of both Northern and Southern Kingdoms. It ends in a place of deep despair and abandonment.

Book 4 (Psalms 90–106) proposes an answer to the confusion brought on by exile: it goes back to earlier and much more stable times. That's why Book 4 begins with a psalm of Moses (Psalm 90). The implication is that the exiles should look back to an earlier time in their story to find grounding. They shouldn't look back to the Davidic monarchy, even with its bold (but ultimately failed) promises. They should look back to a time *before the kingship*. They should look back to God, to the covenant, to the divine promises offered prior to the people's entrance into the Promised Land.

The symbolic turn to the distant past is given its force, not only in Psalm 90's appeal to Moses, but through a series of psalms called the *Yahweh Melek* psalms (Pss 93, 95–99), a phrase which translates to "Yahweh is King." The concentration on divine kingship confronts readers with what should be their true allegiance ... not David, not human kings and earthly kingdoms, but Yahweh.

It's important not to over-spiritualize this as a "we need to return to our first love" sort of thing. Set within the exilic period, there was no other king to choose! The *only option* was Yahweh. It is a very practical conclusion. Book 4 attempted to instill some hope in light of the circumstances. And what better hope than to ascribe kingship to the divine.

Book 5 (Psalms 107–150) brings Psalms, and its narrative arc, to a close. Book 5 begins with an intentional and highly symbolic, poetic regathering of Israel and Judah after the exile. Psalm 107 opens,

> O give thanks to the LORD, for he is good;
>   for his steadfast love endures forever.
> Let the redeemed of the LORD say so,
>   those he redeemed from trouble
>   and gathered in from the lands,
>   from the east and from the west,
>   from the north and from the south. (vv. 1–3)

God is bringing the exiles home.

The rest of Book 5 instructs and rehabilitates its readers, moving them thematically from the failures of the past (Books 1–3) to the re-enthronement of Yahweh (Book 4) to "the glad abandonment of praise" (Book 5), to use Brueggemann's phrase. David is reintroduced here, perhaps signaling the rise of a future Davidic king. It's not a remembrance of a past figure. The people must look ahead, and they must keep in mind their past failures, the trauma of exile, and the rightful kingship of Yahweh.

All told, some readers believe Psalms is ordered to tell Israel's story from the time of the united monarchy under David's leadership to the kingdom's division into two political entities, Israel and Judah, to their eventual destructions, exiles, returns, and the hope of a reconstituted divine kingship.[6]

Revisiting the Date of Psalms

In my estimation, both of these approaches to Psalms are pretty compelling, and as we ministers like to say, "They both preach!"

For Brueggemann, the book of Psalms, and its diversity, represents the diversity of our lives. He knows he is providing an external framework that was not originally intended by the authors/editors of Psalms. His is a "pastoral approach." As such, it doesn't really need to be substantiated. It only needs to be deemed useful. He proposes the book's chaotic movement (in terms of genres) as a picture of the life of faith, both then and now, and the regular experience of seasons of orientation, disorientation, and new orientation.

Viewing the book of Psalms as an intentionally edited collection (as a "playlist" or "mixtape" that has been ordered to create a mood and tell a story) is a bit more difficult to substantiate. But it does seem that the book's editors are trying to say *something* to its readers—from Psalms' division into five books, to the similar doxological statements appended to the end of each book, to the intentional placement of the Psalms' introduction and conclusion, to the presence/absence of David at various points in the book and what that communicates. The narrative I've outlined makes a lot of sense when you look at the book

---

[6] For more on a narrative reading of the "books" of Psalms, deClaissé-Walford's, *Introduction to the Psalms* (pages 129–44), is an excellent entry point.

from 30,000 feet, even if we can't buy into the intentional placement of *every* psalm.

However you choose to think about the final form of Psalms, here's a takeaway we haven't really discussed yet: Psalms as a collection is at least as old as the exile. We know this because the exile is assumed in some psalms, meaning it is also assumed by readers of the finished, edited collection. For exilic and post-exilic readers, then, Psalms *looks back* on the Davidic monarchy, its eventual division into two separate kingdoms, their eventual destruction by foreign powers—Israel by Assyria in 722 BCE and Judah by Babylon in 586 BCE—and the overwhelming tragedy of exile, the destruction of the Jerusalem Temple, and the decimation of their centralized religious system. All of this would naturally call the exilic and post-exilic community's covenant with God into question and color how they read and used Psalms.

Readers' collective memory served as the potent background from which communities of faith were voicing the prayers, praises, petitions, and thanksgivings in Psalms. To put an even finer point on it, communities of faith were constantly having to reimagine its poems in new and—at least in the shadow of the exile—potentially devastating contexts. An individual poem that evoked a pre-exilic or "Davidic" context, then, demanded exilic readers "update" it in order to make use of it. Is God still good? Will God answer? Will God deliver? Will our "core testimony" ever be true again? Will a new David really come?

Modern readers seeking to *use Psalms* must take up this interpretive task as well.

CHAPTER EIGHT

The God(s) of the Psalms

Now that you are ready to win friends and influence people by speaking intelligently on Psalms' background—its history, its authorship, its many literary genres and social settings, its poetic artistry, its formation as a collection, and some of the various approaches to reading the book—let's turn our attention to its theology.

As I mentioned at the outset, my approach in this section will be to focus on the theology of certain psalms. Psalms is a diverse collection of poetry written at different times by different authors in different genres to address different needs in different contexts. I really can't stress that enough. Not only is it an important baseline description of the psalms' content, it also carries some pretty significant interpretive weight. To expect a uniform and monolithic theology from the book's many compositions will most likely lead to strained readings. It will also mute the theological divergences between psalms. So let's not think of what follows as "general theological themes that are held equally throughout Psalms by all of its many contributors." Rather, when we discuss the theology of, say, Psalm 82 … it's just that, the theology of Psalm 82.

As we head into this section of the book, I'd also warn against expecting a stereotypical, modern-day, "churchy" theology from Psalms. [Read: it's going to get weird.] Remember our discussion of Sheol and the afterlife in Chapter Two? Here's a quick refresher just in case you forgot: at a certain point in their history, ancient Israelites thought that when you died, you went to Sheol. And that's fine. But

Sheol functions for contemporary readers as a remnant of ancient theological thinking.

Psalms contains a number of ancient theological concepts that were eventually rejected or forgotten or simply overlooked, and this makes its poems really fascinating as part of a historical record of how people *used to think*. I don't bring this up to disparage the ancient mind or to flaunt our supposed intellectual development. We definitely don't have it all figured out either! In fact, contemporary theology continues to develop (just like we see happening throughout the pages of Scripture). I simply want to reinforce that the theological commitments in Psalms are sometimes notably different to those of modern readers.

To get us going, I'll give you another Sheol-type example. And it's an important one. You might even say that this example stands at the core of ancient Israel's (and every other ancient culture's) theological thinking.

How Many Gods Are There?

This may come as a surprise, but the concept of "monotheism" was a relative latecomer in the world of the Hebrew Bible. Just so we are all on the same page, monotheism is a fancy scholarly word for the belief in the *existence* of one god. Note, belief in the existence of one god is not the same as a commitment to the *worship* of one god (also called monolatry or henotheism). The worship of one god is expected throughout the Hebrew Bible. And at times, so is the *existence of other* gods.

In my experience, many modern readers miss the remnants in the biblical text where other gods were thought to exist. This may be due to a flattening of the development of beliefs in the Bible. Many seem to proceed on the assumption that the things they think now are included unilaterally and uniformly in all parts of the Bible. Psalms challenges this, however, as it provides ample evidence of a dominant cultural belief in the existence of many gods. Here are some of the clearest examples:

> There is none like you *among the gods*, O LORD,
>   nor are there any works like yours. (Ps 86:8)

> For the LORD is a great God,
>   and a great King *above all gods*. (Ps 95:3)

> For great is the LORD, and greatly to be praised;
>   he is to be revered *above all gods*. (Ps 96:4)

> All worshippers of images are put to shame,
>   those who make their boast in worthless idols;
>   *all gods* bow down before him.
> …
> For you, O LORD, are most high over all the earth;
>   you are exalted *far above all gods*. (Ps 97:7, 9)

> For I know that the LORD is great;
>   our Lord is *above all gods*. (Ps 135:5)

One might be tempted to read these lines as nothing more than poetic hyperbole. But the plurality of gods isn't included here for dramatic effect. Many of the psalmists *assumed* the existence of other gods. In fact, to say that the God of Israel is to be revered "above all gods" (or something similar) would make no sense in a context where other gods weren't believed to exist. The image depends upon it.

The point the psalmists are making is that their God is *better than any of the other gods*. Their God is *the only god* out of all the gods in existence who is worthy of worship. In other words, these psalms are demonstrating a commitment to monolatry/henotheism, not monotheism. One of the reasons underlying this conclusion is the fact that monotheism wasn't an option at this time—it hadn't developed yet!

The God of Israel was thought to be one among many gods in existence. To propose otherwise would have been unthinkable in the context these psalms were written.

Monolatry, on the other hand, was well-known and well-accepted throughout the Hebrew Bible. It underlines the battle royal between Yahweh and the Egyptian gods in the early chapters of Exodus ... and the Ten Commandments' opening dictum that the people "not have any gods before Yahweh" ... and the incessant demand in the book of Deuteronomy and in the Prophets for the people to remove their idols and worship Yahweh alone.

What I find interesting is that Israel's theological belief about the *existence* of other gods—a belief that would eventually be outdated (or "wrong")—wasn't corrected by later editorial hands. When monotheism finally developed, no one went back to erase all the talk of "multiple gods." The "many gods exist but only one deserves worship" texts in Psalms (and elsewhere) are still there like a vestigial organ demonstrating Israel's evolutionary theological progress.

What we have in these passages in Psalms, then, are the remnants of a past theological age, an early development in Israel's thinking that has become outdated.

The Divine Boardroom

Another example of belief in the existence of multiple gods is the description of what scholars call the "divine council." Psalm 82, for instance, begins:

> God has taken his place in the divine council;
>   in the midst of the gods he holds judgment ... (v. 1)

Because this picture is so foreign, I'll update it using terms we are more likely to understand.

Imagine a heavenly boardroom, complete with a rich mahogany conference table, high-back leather rolling chairs, golden name plates at each seat, and a 120-inch screen where the attendees can project their fancy PowerPoint presentations. At the end of the table sits the council's chairperson, Yahweh, who is flanked on all sides by other members of the board—the lesser gods and divine aides in Yahweh's employ.

This is the image in Psalm 82. It's a meeting of upper-level executives. Yahweh is seated at the head of the table, and calls the meeting with the team of "lesser gods" to order. It seems crazy, but you are probably familiar with the image, even if unknowingly.

A divine council is featured, for example, in the well-known "wager scene" in the introduction to the book of Job: "One day the heavenly beings came to present themselves before the LORD, and Satan[1] also came among them..." (Job 1:6). The "heavenly beings" who appear before Yahweh are literally called, "the sons of God," in Hebrew *(bene ha'elohim)*. I imagine when we read "heavenly beings," we think of angels, but that misses the sense of the phrase. These are lesser gods—the executives who attend the divine council. We tend not to go here because (1) the concept of a divine council is not part of our cultural language and (2) we have probably imported monotheism ("there aren't other gods!") back into the text when it isn't appropriate to do so.

---

[1] In Hebrew, it's not "Satan" who joins Yahweh in the divine council, it's "the Satan" (*hasatan* in Hebrew). It means something like, "the adversary" or "the accuser" or "the prosecuting attorney." It's not a proper name, it's a description of one of the lesser gods in the council. The concept of "Satan" developed much later, sometime before the New Testament period—which is why we see Satan as a character in the New Testament. The dominant cultural caricature of Satan—in red tights with a pitchfork—developed even later than that, sometime in the Medieval period.

The Theology of Psalm 82

In Psalm 82, Yahweh uses the opportunity presented by the divine council to lambaste the other gods for their participation in injustice and their apparent lack of concern for the weak, the orphan, the lowly and destitute.

Before I provide the text, you should know there is a lot of discussion in Psalms scholarship on who is speaking in the psalm. The reading I have adopted identifies the psalmist's voice as a frame for the poem. The rest of it is spoken by Yahweh.[2]

> *The psalmist:* God has taken his place in the divine council;
>   in the midst of the gods he holds judgment:
>
> *Yahweh:* "How long will you [lesser deities] judge unjustly
>   and show partiality to the wicked?
>   *Selah*
>
> Give justice to the weak and the orphan;
>   maintain the right of the lowly and the destitute.
> Rescue the weak and the needy;
>   deliver them from the hand of the wicked."
>
> They have neither knowledge nor understanding;
>   they walk around in darkness;
>   all the foundations of the earth are shaken.
>
> I say, "You are gods [Note: Yahweh is still talking to the lesser deities in the divine council],
>   children of the Most High, all of you;

---

[2] See, for example, Robert Alter, *The Book of Psalms: A Translation with Commentary* (New York: W. W. Norton & Company, 2007), 291–93.

nevertheless, you shall die like mortals,
and fall like any prince."

The psalmist: Rise up, O God, judge the earth,
for all the nations belong to you!

Yahweh pronounces judgment on the lesser gods who are present at the council meeting, culminating in a proposed death sentence ("you shall die like mortals"). Before I explain that, notice this aspect of the psalm's teaching: the advocacy for and enactment of justice and the protection of the poor and marginalized are divine acts, which, if left unaccomplished, render one unfit for office. The gods' failure in this regard occasions the passionate plea from the psalmist,

Rise up, O God, judge the earth,
for all the nations belong to you! (v. 8)

Psalm 82 is a prayer for Yahweh to do the things a god should do, namely, promote justice, fight for the oppressed, and tear down the powerful.

For the perceptive reader, two things should be clear. First, the theological belief informing Psalm 82, particularly its affirmation of the existence of other gods and their potential function in the divine council, is operative here, but it is not endorsed throughout the Bible. In fact, some propose that Psalm 82 and its divine death sentence ("you shall die like mortals") provides an important landmark in this theological development. The death of the gods signals the movement from polytheism to monotheism in the thought world of ancient Israel.

Whether that is right or not, what we have here is a culturally-embedded snapshot of a particular psalmist's theology at a specific moment in time. When we approach Psalms as a whole, we shouldn't be surprised when we are exposed to remnants of ancient theological thinking like all this stuff about divine councils.

Second, the psalm's weird/outdated/ancient ideas do not fully encompass the poem's teaching. What I mean is, Psalm 82's primary theological contribution does not concern the existence of other gods or the activity of the divine council. Those are assumptions the author makes. The more foundational theological point in Psalm 82 is how Yahweh detests the lesser gods' lack of care and concern for the poor and oppressed, and their resultant judgment (perhaps even to death). The divine council is merely the vehicle used to communicate this point.

The psalm teaches that justice matters. Equity matters. Impartiality matters. The poor and the oppressed matter. According to the psalmist, to act as a god *should* is to

> Give justice to the weak and the orphan;
>> maintain the right of the lowly and the destitute.
> Rescue the weak and the needy;
>> deliver them from the hand of the wicked. (vv. 3–4)

And when the gods weren't doing this, they were removed from power. Israel's God, on the other hand, was expected to perform these duties, so the psalmist cried out for God to do what they believed a god should.

Not What You Expected, Right?

Reading Psalms theologically demands our engagement with ancient ideas, some of which we have come to reject. Within American Christianity, you don't hear many sermons affirming divine councils and the existence of "lesser gods" and monolatry (with the accompanying ancient belief that other gods really existed). But those concepts are *in the Bible*, which is pretty wild. These are culturally-embedded theological snapshots, and too often, we miss them entirely.

CHAPTER NINE

Sea Monsters & Dragons

The most popular creation stories in the Bible are undoubtedly the two that appear in the first few chapters of the book of Genesis.[1] Sadly, the *theological* significance of these foundational stories is often overshadowed in contemporary conversation by scientific concerns. But Genesis is not a *scientific* text. It doesn't seek to answer our questions of origins. Genesis is a *theological* text, and if we are to understand its theology rightly, we must first place its stories in their decidedly ancient contexts.

It's the same with Psalms. It also has quite a bit to say about creation and is, as we've already seen, also set in decidedly ancient contexts. Focusing on "the science" of Psalms will lead us too far afield, causing us to miss the *theological* point.

In this chapter, we will look at two poems, Psalm 104 and Psalm 74, in that order. Both of these psalms (and their included poetic images) are quite similar to the depictions of creation offered in Genesis. They "live in the same world" or "breathe the same air." The depictions of creation in Genesis and Psalms, in other words, share certain, non-scientific/mythic conceptions of the world ... like when they talk about sea monsters!

---

[1] For more information on the creation stories in Genesis, see Peter Enns and Jared Byas, *Genesis for Normal People*, and Peter Enns, *The Evolution of Adam: What the Bible Does and Doesn't Say about Human Origins*, 10th anniversary ed. (Grand Rapids, MI: Brazos Press, 2021).

Creation and Chaos

To set this up, let's think about the first creation story in Genesis for a bit (Gen 1:1–2:4a). In the first few verses, we learn that "when God began creating,"[2] the earth was formless and empty. These are important details. As many scholars note, the story in Genesis does not describe God creating the earth out of nothing. That phenomenon, called creation *ex nihilo*, occurs elsewhere in the Bible (see Heb 11:3). In Genesis 1, the earth was already there. Where it came from isn't the point. As readers, we are asked to accept a formless and empty earth already in existence. This description sets up the creative activity in the chapter. Because the earth is formless and empty, God forms it (days one to three) and fills it (days four to six).

We also learn early on in Genesis 1, before the forming and filling begin, that darkness was over "the deep." Just to be clear, God didn't create "the deep" either. Like the earth, it just … was. A large part of God's creative work in Genesis 1 is dealing with stuff that was already there. God takes this preexisting blob of watery matter and separates the seas from the dry land. God also separates the "water above" from the "water below." To help us understand just how ancient this description is, the author says God placed a dome or an expanse—a ceiling of sorts—in the sky to keep the "water above" up there somewhere.[3]

Clearly, this cosmological description doesn't fit with what we now know about the world from a scientific viewpoint. Genesis 1 is an *ancient* and *mythic* description of creation. It highlights God's preparatory work to make the earth habitable for fish, birds, land animals, creeping things, and eventually, humans, like when Bob Ross first paints a beautiful wooded backdrop before adding a "happy squirrel."

---

[2] This phrase is a pretty good translation of the opening phrase of Genesis—not the traditional, "In the beginning, God created," but "When God began creating…"

[3] Fun fact: the water above was later released in Genesis, in the story of the Flood, when the "floodgates" in the dome were opened.

Theologically, the forming in days one through three and the filling in days four through six is God taking what was *chaotic* and *taming* it … which is a huge point in the creation narrative in its ancient setting.

Back then, descriptive elements like "formlessness" and "emptiness" and most terms about "seas" and "water" and "the deep" represented threats to creation. They were things to be feared in the ancient mind because they were understood as forces of chaos. We see this, not only in Genesis, but in other ancient Near Eastern stories as well. The Babylonian creation story, *Enuma Elish*, which features Marduk defeating Tiamat (a water goddess), and the Canaanite stories about Baal (the storm god) defeating Yamm (the sea god) are good examples. The mythological motif of the primordial waters as potential threats was "in the air" in the ancient world. Unlike these other stories, though, God simply orders the chaos in Genesis 1. When God's spirit hovers non-violently over the "waters" in the early verses of Genesis 1, it's a power move. It's as if God is saying to the primordial waters, "You go where I tell you to go." If the chaos of "the deep" was threatening initially, God tamed it.

This is where sea monsters come in.

If you're thinking, "I've read Genesis 1 a few times, and I don't remember any sea monsters," you're probably right. Part of the reason for that is how the Hebrew word *tannin* (plural: *tanninim*) is translated in our English Bibles. It's often rendered "great creatures of the sea" or something like that. The NRSV, however, goes all in with the phrase, "the great sea monsters." Even here, I'm guessing most modern readers would immediately make sense of the phrase by equating it with sharks, barracudas, electric eels, sperm whales, the thing in *Finding Nemo* with the light bulb on top of its head so it can eat other, smaller fish in the dark. Stuff like that. Stuff we know. We don't usually conclude, "Great sea monsters, huh? I guess this is when God created the Loch Ness Monster." But actually, in its ancient Near Eastern context, Nessie wouldn't be too far off from what was envisioned.

In the ancient world, sea monsters were mythical creatures that functioned as forces of chaos, as agents of fear and disorder. They lived in the dangerous (and pre-existent) waters of "the deep,"[4] and they were, in a word, a problem. We could reduce it to the formula: sea monsters = bad. Again, this is not unique to Genesis. We see these figures in other ancient Near Eastern stories too.

But, here's the kicker: in Genesis 1, the sea monsters are *created* beings, placed pretty casually in a long list of other created beings on day five. The implied threat of the *tanninim* is effectively neutralized because God made them and placed them in their habitat. In fact, these monsters are pronounced "good," along with everything else God made.

Take all of this into account and the creation story in Genesis 1 becomes a subtle argument against other ancient cultures' creation stories. It is claiming that the God of Israel was in complete control. (This theology is informed by monolatry. Other gods *existed*, but Israel's God was *better*.) Israel's God tamed chaos—the waters, the deep—and not only that, Israel's God *created* other potential threats, such as sea monsters, and called them "good." It's a powerful theological message stating that the God of Israel is not afraid of the sea or the stuff in it.

When God Creates Sea Monsters as Pets

The poet of Psalm 104 makes a similar theological point in their appeal to creation. The goal of the poem is doxological. It is meant to evoke praise to "the God to whom [creation] witnesses."[5]

This is accomplished most clearly in the psalmist's commentary on God's creation of the great sea monster, Leviathan. The psalmist writes,

---

[4] In the Babylonian story, *Enuma Elish* (we'll talk more about this soon), the goddess Tiamat is a water god, represented as watery chaos. Some scholars like to draw a parallel between her name, Tiamat, and the similar sounding Hebrew word for "the deep," *tehom*.

[5] Jon D. Levenson, *Creation and the Persistence of Evil: The Jewish Drama of Divine Omnipotence* (Princeton, NJ: Princeton University Press, 1988), 57–58.

O Lord, how manifold are your works!
> In wisdom you have made them all;
> the earth is full of your creatures.
Yonder is the sea, great and wide,
> creeping things innumerable are there,
> living things both small and great.
There go the ships,
> and Leviathan that you formed to sport in it. (vv. 24–26)

Leviathan was a specific sea monster, a specific *tannin*, which was, again, a representative of the forces of chaos in the world. As such, it was feared. The theological point of Leviathan's creation is very clear in Psalm 104—Leviathan was formed by God to be a plaything, a pet for God's amusement. It wasn't threatening or scary or unpredictable. It was cute. God created Leviathan for fun.

Both Genesis 1 and Psalm 104 are distinct when compared to other cultures' creation accounts in that God creates and orders the world without resorting to violence. Other extra-biblical stories include graphic descriptions of battles between the gods as contributing factors or causes of the origins of the earth and humanity. For example, in *Enuma Elish*, Marduk defeats the water goddess, Tiamat, and filets her body. He sets one part of her carcass in the sky to serve as a ceiling to keep the "water above" out of the earth below. The same image appears in Genesis, but God simply creates a ceiling or dome to keep the "water above" up there somewhere. No fighting or fileting lesser gods was necessary.

Creation, in *Enuma Elish* and other stories from the ancient Near East, is the product of warfare. It's bloody. It's violent. It involves a struggle. But in Genesis 1 and Psalm 104, chaos is tamed by God's speech, by God's presence, by the limits God places on potentially threatening entities. There is no battle in these biblical creation stories, and that's part of the point: Israel's God is different. Israel's God is unthreatened. Israel's God didn't need to go to war against other gods.

Israel's God tames chaos with a word. As a result, Israel's God alone is worthy of worship.

When Psalms brings up creation, this seems to be the point—creation proves the power of God and the proper response is worship.

But sometimes "chaos" seems to break through. Sometimes the world is disordered and at odds with any notion of divine control. To use the image of sea monsters, sometimes "Leviathan" breaches the water and shows its big terrible teeth.

When God Crushes the Heads of Sea Monsters

The period of Babylonian exile in the 6th century BCE is a prime example of the in-breaking of chaos. In this event, foreign invaders destroyed Jerusalem and its Temple, and they displaced many of the people from the Promised Land. It would have felt like a theological undoing of God's covenant, leaving the exiles to wonder, "what now?" For folks in this context, any talk of Leviathan as God's "pet" probably wouldn't have resonated with its audience. Leviathan, and the chaos it represented, was on the loose.

Some psalmists accommodated, adapting the imagery that appears in Psalm 104. A good example is Psalm 74.

Psalm 74 is a community lament that many scholars believe was written in response to the fall of Jerusalem and the Babylonian exile (i.e., right when Leviathan was wreaking havoc). Because the psalmist's enemies were winning, the psalm includes a petition for God to act. And it uses some familiar images to convey the point,

> Yet God my King is from of old,
>   working salvation in the earth.
> You divided the sea by your might;
>   you broke the heads of the dragons (*tanninim*) in the waters.
> You crushed the heads of Leviathan;
>   you gave him as food for the creatures of the wilderness.

> You cut openings for springs and torrents;
>> you dried up ever-flowing streams.
> Yours is the day, yours also the night;
>> you established the luminaries and the sun.
> You have fixed all the bounds of the earth;
>> you made summer and winter. (vv. 12–17)

We can see some of the standard creation language in use here. God divides the waters. God establishes the luminaries. God sets up the borders of the earth. God rules over the seasons. There are some familiar "characters" too: the sea, the waters, the *tanninim* (translated in the NRSV as "dragons"!), and our old friend, Leviathan. But unlike Genesis 1 and Psalm 104, the psalmist describes God's dominance over these entities, particularly, the sea monsters, in violent terms. During creation, the psalmist says, God broke the dragons' heads. God crushed the heads (plural) of Leviathan.[6] God fought against chaos in an attempt to subdue it, and in the psalmist's adaptation of the creation story, God won.[7]

For a people suffering displacement, a remembrance like this would be a powerful witness of what happened, and what is possible, maybe more so than Psalm 104 and its depiction of Leviathan as a pet. The psalmist tells the story to remind the audience that God has tamed chaos before … and that God can tame chaos again. Walter Brueggemann and William H. Bellinger Jr. write, "The angst is palpable in this prayer that cajoles God to deal with the crisis. The prayer petitions the covenant God to act in the tradition of the Creation, in which God brought order and life out of chaos."[8]

---

[6] I'll include this just for fun: some see resonances between the many-headed Leviathan and the many-headed dragon in the book of Revelation.

[7] The violent battle imagery of Psalm 74 might also evoke an allusion to the exodus event. The crossing of the Red Sea could also be seen as a re-enactment of the mythic battle against "the sea" and "the deep" and "sea monsters." See Isaiah 51:9–11.

[8] Brueggemann and Bellinger, *Psalms* (2014), 324.

The Theologies of Creation in Psalms 104 and 74

The psalmists' use of creation themes in Psalms 104 and 74 is a theologically potent image, understandable in its fullness only when it is set in its ancient context. Both poems assume the forces of chaos are a threat. In Psalm 104, the threat was neutralized before it started—Leviathan, it says, was created as God's plaything. In Psalm 74, chaos has been unleashed, and God needs to tame it again. The psalmist appeals to the past, but in different terms. God's taming of chaos was achieved by breaking the heads of dragons and crushing the heads of Leviathan. Because of the situation facing the psalmist, non-violence was out of the question.

Both poems utilize images of God taming chaos to affirm an important piece of Israel's core theology: in creation, God demonstrated power and control. The logic is, if things get out of hand, God is able to provide order once again. As Beth LaNeel Tanner notes, "[U]nderlying these pleas is a confidence that these pleas will ultimately be successful."[9] God has done it before ... God can do it again.

For an ancient audience, a reminder of the past would provide some comfort in the face of uncertainty, struggle, and threat. It serves as a testimony to who God is, or, as in Psalm 74, who God could (and *should*) be. In either case, the psalm's witness to past events, retold in all of their mythic glory, is meant to evoke praise and trust in the mind of the reader because of what God has done in the past.

As we will see, God's past actions are very important in Psalms, and it's not limited to creation. It's all of it. Everything that God *has already done* serves as the foundation for the book's ongoing and various calls to trust. In other words, Psalms doesn't just claim that God is "good" and leave it at that. It seeks to *prove* God was/is/will be good through many and varied appeals to the past.

---

[9] Nancy deClaissé-Walford, Rolf A. Jacobson, and Beth LaNeel Tanner, *The Book of Psalms* (The New International Commentary on the Old Testament; Grand Rapids, MI: William B. Eerdmans Publishing Company, 2014), 601.

CHAPTER TEN

"For Yahweh's *Acts of Faithfulness* Endure Forever"

In the last chapter, I argued that psalmists often appeal to God's past actions in order to encourage trust in the present. That's why they talk about "the deep" and mythical sea monsters such as Leviathan. It's a reminder that God has tamed chaos before, and by that logic, when the need arises God can do it again.

There's a common refrain that occurs throughout Psalms that will help us anchor this theological tenet about God's past actions informing the people's present trust. In our English translations, the refrain is typically rendered, "for Yahweh's steadfast love endures forever." For many modern readers, however, the point is missed.

I Could Sing of Your *Hesed* Forever

My upbringing was very "churchy." In my experience, the phrase "steadfast love" is one of those well-known Bible phrases that congregants have heard, maybe even prayed or sung, but no one ever really explains. Perhaps it's assumed we can piece its meaning together based on our knowledge of the English language. That approach works in some instances, but when you bring a loaded term like "love" into the conversation, we import too much of our own cultural baggage—from the rom-coms we've seen on Netflix to the Luther Vandross singles we've crooned in the car. Working from that cultural lens, we might be prone to construct a strange sort of divine romance, where God's love for us "endures forever."

The Hebrew term rendered "steadfast love" is *hesed*, and its intended meaning goes well beyond sentimentality. It refers to "acts of commitment" or "acts of faithfulness." God's love, in other words, is measured not by what God feels, but by what God *has done*. In Psalms, *hesed* is an observable divine activity that consistently works on Israel's behalf.

Psalm 136 is a good example. It begins,

> O give thanks to the LORD, because he is good,
>> because [Yahweh's] *acts of commitment* (Hebrew: *hesed*) endure
> forever. (v. 1; my translation)

As my translation makes clear, the psalmist is not celebrating some amorphous relational concept. Neither is the psalmist prodding the worshipping community to give thanks on the basis of a detached claim about who or what God is, namely, because "God's character is good." There's more to it. Give thanks to Yahweh, the psalmist says, because Yahweh is *demonstrably* good. Yahweh has shown up in the past. Yahweh's "love" has been evident. To use a well-known turn of phrase, Yahweh's love is a love that "does."

Psalm 136 provides a laundry list of evidence: creation, the exodus, the sustaining of Israel in the wilderness, the giving of land to Israel. In fact, in each poetic line, the psalmist briefly recalls an act of God in the first colon, and then sounds the refrain, "for [Yahweh's] acts of commitment endure forever," in the second colon. All told, the rhythm of a rehearsal of past actions followed by the repeated refrain focusing on God's *hesed* provides an onslaught of positive evidence of divine acts of love and commitment for the reader. As such, the goodness of God (and the readers' hoped-for trust in God) is proven in the things God has done, the ways God has acted on behalf of God's people. When you take the entire psalm in, the intonation is clear: celebrate the past—all the things God has done, all the ways in which God's *hesed* has been demonstrated—and trust that this divine activity will continue here and now.

Psalm 136 is one of the so-called "historical psalms," but it is not merely a remembering of past events for their own sake. The psalmist's recollection has an instructive edge to it. It's reminding worshippers who their God is and what their God has done, and it's teaching them to trust that their God will be this type of God and do these sorts of things again. The goal is comparable to what we've seen in psalms that appeal to creation for a similar purpose (e.g., Psalms 104 and 74).

For the psalmist, the past informs the present … and, precisely because "Yahweh's *acts of commitment (hesed)* endure forever," it informs readers how they might approach life in the here and now and the yet to come.

More Stories of a Faithful God

Psalm 107 is another instructive example for understanding God's *hesed* as acts that provide tangible evidence of God's commitment. It also shows how the rehearsal of these past events is used as proof of God's ongoing involvement in the lives of the people. The poem begins with the same opening line as Psalm 136:

> O give thanks to the LORD, because he is good,
> > because [Yahweh's] *acts of commitment* (Hebrew: *hesed*) endure forever. (Ps 107:1)

This opening line is especially important for the psalmist given the poem's apparent setting in the post-exilic period. For a community that is suffering the sorts of theological and practical (!) setbacks brought about by their displacement, an appeal to what God has done to prove God's ongoing commitment is of the utmost importance.

They need a witness to something other than exile and destruction and abandonment.

In the experience of exile, the "sea monster" has shown its teeth, but as we've seen, God has demonstrated the ability to tame chaos in the past. And according to the psalmist of Psalm 107, God has done it again. As a result, the psalmist invites those who have experienced divine deliverance to "say so"—those whom God has "redeemed from the hand of the foe, and gathered them from the lands, from the east and west, from north and south"[1] (vv. 2–3). What follows in the psalm is a stylized compilation of four vignettes detailing God's deliverance of formerly displaced people, some of whom were wandering in the wilderness, some were imprisoned, some were in trouble because of their misdeeds, and some were in danger on the sea. As we've come to expect from a thanksgiving psalm, all of these people groups retell their story: they cried out to God, God heard them, and then God responded positively. The stories follow the expected pattern of need–petition–rescue. Because these people have been "redeemed" from their oppressors, they tell their stories and, effectively, add them to the ongoing list of deeds demonstrating God's *hesed*.

Again, the point is not merely to tell these stories in corporate worship. These four stories, especially when viewed collectively, teach the worshipping community an important lesson, clarified by the poem's concluding instruction,

> Let those who are wise give heed to these things,
>   and consider Yahweh's *acts of commitment* (Hebrew: *hesed*).
> (Ps 107:43)

---

[1] Most English translations follow a suggestion made by the editors of the standard, critical Hebrew text. They "emend" (or change) the text, so that it provides all four points on a compass: east, west, north, and south. However, the Hebrew text and its manuscript traditions do not provide any basis for such a change. The text clearly says, "east, west, north, and the sea," which actually fits the content of the psalm. The final story of rescue (the final testimony) features the divine deliverance of sailors in danger on the *sea*.

I have a theory about psalms like Psalm 107 and Psalm 136.[2] Here it is in a nutshell: retelling stories of God's faithfulness in ancient Israelite worship was important, and it should have had an impact on listeners. It should have shaped them ethically. It should have transformed their character. It should have affirmed who the community of faith thought God was and how they expected God to act. It should have inspired trust and faith and hope in their hearers. Because God did these things back then, a listener might be inclined to believe God will keep doing things like this. Stories of divine deliverance, in other words, affirmed Israel's "core testimony" and the expectations that came with it.

We can move pretty confidently in this interpretive direction because these poems were not just an offering *to God*. They were a communal witness *to the psalm's audience* and *to generations of worshippers since*. They argue, "If God did that for us back then, and if God did this for that person more recently, maybe God can do it for me too."

And it's all tied up in the celebrations of God's "steadfast love."

Hesed Does

God's *hesed* underlines a lot of Psalms' poetry, even when the psalmists' are calling God's character (and God's actions) into question. In the lament psalms, for example, the psalmists are saying there are no tangible acts of faithfulness on God's part to speak of. They have been abandoned. They are alone. They are threatened by enemies or sickness or impending disaster. Their world is a chaotic mess.

Still, the lament psalms *usually* turn to an affirmation of trust by the end of their petition. This literary shift is part of the stereotypical form of the genre. It works like this—in lament, psalmists decry their current situation. Then they call God to task. They demand God act on their behalf as God has acted (either for them or for others) in the

---

[2] I wrote a book on it if you're interested. It's called *The Storied Ethics of the Thanksgiving Psalms* (LHBOTS 658; New York: Bloomsbury, 2017).

past. And then they turn to trust. Such a move is possible because of psalms like Psalm 136 and Psalm 107, both of which provide relevant and powerful responses to the sort of testimony offered in the lament psalms. They both provide the end of the story—what happens after lament and petition and plea. They argue, "Despite what it looks like, God *has been* faithful. I've seen it. Listen to these stories and consider, why not here? Why not now? Why not for you?"

When we read the refrain, "for Yahweh's steadfast love endures forever," I hope we hear it as the ancient Israelites would have—not as something overly sentimental, but as a poignant reminder that God's *hesed* does.

CHAPTER ELEVEN

The (Still) Costly Loss of Lament

I know I said I would strive for objectivity, but I want to ask for a reprieve for the next two chapters. I'd rather not be too detached when we talk about lament and the extreme circumstances that inspire it. I'd also like to get a little personal, if you don't mind. Is that OK? I guess you can't really say "no," but I'll choose to take your silence as enthusiastic affirmation.

Being a minister is hard. Being a minister in a social-media dependent, highly politically-divisive, fear-driven, conspiracy-accepting, mid/post (I think?)-COVID-19 American context is *really* hard. In response, ministers in my faith tradition are quitting in droves.[1] And I have to be honest, some days that sounds lovely. Financial concerns, identity issues, and (thankfully, this much more spiritual-sounding reason) my deep love for the people in our faith community, have all kept me plodding along throughout our country's last two presidential elections, a global pandemic, my own personal existential crises (plural),

---

[1] My broad ministerial context is Baptist. Carol McEntyre and Pam Durso have written about the increasing number of resignations among Baptist ministers in "Leaving Church: So Many Baptist Resignations," *Baptist News Global*, November 30, 2021, https://baptistnews.com/article/leaving-church-so-many-baptist-resignations

and a constant mid-to-low grade depression. "I am in the Pit, Lord! Hear my prayer!"

If you are an attentive reader, you may have noticed one glaring absence from my list of things that make ministry (and life in general) so damn hard. I would characterize it this way: the neverending barrage of unspeakable tragedies that headline our 24-hour news cycle for a few days before being replaced by other, different unspeakable tragedies. Even as I wrote this chapter, I took a break, picked up my phone, and started scrolling through Instagram. Flanked by sports highlights and a video from one of my favorite internet guitarists, there was a post about the rising frequency of American school shootings in which the shooter was a child. It's inescapable and overwhelming. As a minister, I have often felt an unspoken pressure to address all of these tragedies in some meaningful way—to provide hope and light for a community of people that are hurting or, as is often the case, a community of people who are slowly becoming desensitized to horrific happenings that, each one, should cause us to question the fate of humanity. But here's the thing: if that's one of my pastoral responsibilities, I usually have no words to offer.

Lamenting the Costly Loss of Lament

The lament psalms offer a fitting response to my confused silence. As the most common type of psalm in the entire collection, their overwhelming presence should encourage readers to raise their voice in petition and protest whenever injustice arises. If words are needed, perhaps these time-honored, community-approved, honest and impassioned pleas are the ones.

In some faith communities, such encouragement is not needed: lament is not offered infrequently via a Facebook post written in response to yet another national tragedy, it is a "breath prayer," arising naturally and consistently. For example, when I was struggling to put something into words following the deaths of Ahmaud Arbery,

Breonna Taylor and George Floyd, Rev. Otis Moss III and his team at Trinity United Church of Christ produced a seamless and visually stunning "sermonic movie." In it, Moss powerfully outlined America's racist past and present, calling upon the questions raised by the psalmist—questions raised over two millennia ago—as his guiding light,

> It is the poet of the psalms, who raises the question—and it is the word to those of us who are fearful for our children on this day and want to see a better nation rise. It is the word that we all must shout together collectively as citizens of this country, if it is to be the country that God intends it to be. We must wrestle with the question, "How long must I wrestle with these thoughts?" As the psalmist says, "How long must I rest in this sorrow and must it speak from my soul?" The question from the poet is the question every black parent who raises a child must raise within their soul ...[2]

Among other things, Moss seems to suggest that lament is not only a response, it's ongoing. It's perpetual. It is necessary daily language occasioned, in the Black community, by a constant acknowledgement of the wrong in the world and resulting in the consequent demand that God change it.[3]

But in some other faith communities, the public practice of lament has been forsaken, exchanged instead with the offering of contextually tone-deaf praise when a dirge would be more appropriate. Seemingly, this was the approach employed by many white-majority

---

[2] Rev. Dr. Otis Moss III, "The Cross and the Lynching Tree: A Requiem for Ahmaud Arbery," (May 17, 2020), https://www.youtube.com/watch?v=l6985UG0Z3k

[3] I don't mean to imply lament is the only type of prayer that is offered regularly. See Gabby Cudjoe-Wilkes and Andrew Wilkes' *Psalms for Black Lives: Reflections for the Work of Liberation* (Nashville, TN: Upper Room Books, 2022) for an example of how other psalm genres were also used in response to the events of 2020.

faith communities in the US in response to the very same tragedies Moss addressed head on. In addition to an unwillingness to engage "controversial" social issues from the pulpit, to question God, to raise one's voice, to challenge or make demands is deemed inappropriate and, therefore, taken off the table for inclusion in public worship. As a result, when large segments of the world (and, ostensibly, the congregation) are rightfully grieving, these communities choose to close their eyes, lift their hands, and sing about God's goodness.

It is often the case in communities where lament is avoided that individuals grieving incalculable personal loss are subtly (or not so subtly) pressured to get back to normal as quickly as possible. This messaging is often accompanied by theologically-bankrupt but often-used platitudes about "God's plan" or "God's timing" or how your recently deceased loved one is "in a better place."[4] There is no room for lament.

In the mid-1980s, Walter Brueggemann addressed the proclivity toward unacknowledged pain in an essay called "The Costly Loss of Lament."[5] His argument is less, "No one reads laments!" and more "Here's what happens if you participate in a faith community that doesn't read or pray laments" (though, the former is still endemic in some faith communities for reasons outlined earlier). Brueggemann highlights two unfortunate results. First, when a faith community avoids lament, they implicitly diminish the importance of its members' voices and their status in the divine-human dialogue. When this occurs, the community is taught by example to respond to moments of great need with either silence or praise. Lament is not an option. God is too lofty, and our complaints are misplaced and inappropriate.

Second, Brueggemann contends that a faith community that avoids lament doesn't acknowledge the wrong in the(ir) world or demand that

---

[4] For a more fitting theological alternative, see Thomas Jay Oord, *God Can't: How to Believe in God and Love After Tragedy, Abuse, and Other Evils* (Grasmere, ID: SacraSage Press, 2019).

[5] Walter Brueggemann, "The Costly Loss of Lament," *Journal for the Study of the Old Testament* 36 (1986): 57–71.

God change it. Again, the community is taught, largely by example, that the proper recourse is to be quiet or choose praise. Brueggemann writes, "A community of faith that negates laments soon concludes that the hard issues of justice are improper questions to pose at the throne, because the throne seems to be only a place of praise."[6] Consequently, community members are "consigned to anxiety and despair"[7] because the world is envisioned as fixed and God (basically) unapproachable.

Clearly, for some readers, Brueggemann's essay is near-nonsense, not in its conclusions, of course, but in its very premise. "How could one ever *lose* lament? How could people *not demand* God fix what is broken? How could we ever not grieve?" My experience, however, affirms the usefulness of this essay for a broad audience, if not for the theological reasons Brueggemann states (i.e., the diminishment of one's voice and status; the placement of praise over and above lament), then for the privilege and self-involvement some worshippers experience that *allows* them to neglect lament. (We'll revisit this in the next chapter.)

Vindication and Justice

In contrast to the tendency to exclude lament in some communities, Psalms speaks a different word. The editor(s) provided ample room for lament in the collection of ancient Israel's prayers—a resource, we should remind ourselves, that many scholars believe functioned as a guide to order corporate worship. The book's ancient editors, in other words, affirmed the regular, public, communal use of lament.

The inclusion of lament in Psalms also legitimizes a worshipper's unbridled outpouring of their feelings and circumstances. God, apparently, can handle it— whatever it may be—even if the pray-er does not offer the characteristic "turn to trust" that we have come to expect

---

[6] Ibid., 64.
[7] Ibid., 64.

in the lament form. Psalm 88, for example, simply ends with, "You have caused friend and neighbor to shun me; my companions are in darkness" (v. 18). The final colon could also be translated with darkness as the subject: "darkness is my closest friend." At the end of this line, the psalm is over. The curtain closes. The screen fades to black. Credits begin to roll. The psalmist's pain is unrelenting. There is no closure and no resolve. For those who feel this on a visceral level, the absence of praise is wonderfully cathartic. The psalm does not force its audience to rush through their inability to trust. Instead, they are afforded the opportunity to say what they need to say, then simply walk away.

For some of you, that makes perfect sense. You have felt that grief. You have wrestled with darkness or, as the psalm suggests, befriended it. For others, this is not where you live—either currently or perhaps ever. In that case, we would do well to consider this: the gut-wrenching content of Psalm 88, and others laments like it, should encourage readers (and pray-ers) who are "fine" (whatever that entails) to think beyond themselves to those whose situations are characterized by pain and suffering ... and perhaps also systemic historical oppression, political tumult, displacement, war or overwhelming sadness. While I would not want to attempt to reconstruct the situations behind the lament psalms, we are at least safe to conclude that innumerable people in the ancient world and throughout the history of interpretation have offered these psalms in times of sheer desperation. Perhaps this simple (and obvious) fact is enough to inspire their consistent use in public worship. Or, if you are an irreligious person, having no desire to use these psalms, perhaps this reminder is enough to inspire a humanitarian concern and, if possible, action. Someone, somewhere not too far away, *needs* words of lament.

Let's consider Psalm 43 as an example.

Most scholars believe that Psalms 42 and 43 belong together. Formally, they are linked by a similar structure, which, when they are taken together forms three stanzas, each one concluding with a similar version of this refrain:

Why are you cast down, O my soul,
    and why are you disquieted within me?
Hope in God; for I shall again praise him,
      my help and my God. (Ps 42:5–6; also 42:11, 43:5)

I am choosing to focus on the content of Psalm 43 because it can stand on its own, even if it was meant to function as the conclusion to the preceding psalm at some point. But first, a word on Psalm 42.

Psalm 42 is a lament psalm, though its form is a bit odd. It makes no explicit petition. The psalmist outlines their situation, and at the end of Psalm 42, the psalmist debates it internally, attempting to talk themselves into hoping in God. In verse 5c, the psalmist claims, "I will again praise God." Up to this point, they haven't asked for deliverance.

Psalm 43, on the other hand, gets to the asking very quickly. The poem begins with a pointed petition. (This is another reason some people think the poem was added as a complement to Psalm 42. Psalm 43 adds "the ask" that is missing from its predecessor.) The psalmist prays that God would do what God is *supposed* to do, maybe hearkening back to some of those past displays of *hesed* that we discussed in the last chapter. It's as if they are making a case, "Ok, God, you're supposed to be faithful, right? You're supposed to demonstrate acts of commitment, aren't you? Well then, get to it …"

Vindicate me, O God, and defend my cause
    against an ungodly people;
from those who are deceitful and unjust
    deliver me! (Ps 43:1)

The psalmist calls God to act on their behalf, to bring them justice, and to do it now. It's an honest and expressive and, quite frankly, bold petition. And it's exemplary in its potential usefulness for readers, both ancient and modern, who long for vindication.

The psalm ends with the same internal conversation, the same self-talk questioning the psalmist's downcast state, followed by the (mildly) hopeful refrain, "I'm going to praise again … my help and my God." Brueggemann and Bellinger call attention to the final line's use of 1st-person pronouns "*my* help and *my* God" as an important theological statement. It suggests a "concluding hope in relationship with the living God, the God who comes to deliver."[8]

When life goes sideways—for you or for someone in your community or for people you see on your news apps—we need hope like this. We need hope that God will deliver. In the tradition of ancient Israel's lament psalms, we begin by demanding it,

"Vindicate me"

… or "vindicate us"

… or "vindicate the victims of injustice."

But I don't believe we stop here, with a bold ask, with "thoughts and prayers." In the New Testament tradition, this would be no different than the person who, upon seeing someone in need, merely wishes them well (see James 2:14–17). To pray a lament psalm, and to mean it, is to join the fight against injustice or to sit with a sibling who is grieving or to see the wrong in the world and do what we can to fix it.

Listening to Lament

If Psalms has a say in how our public worship is formed, lament is something that needs to be uttered. We need these strong petitions for God to act like God *has* in the past, like God is *supposed to* in the here and now. We need honest self-talk that admits our spirits are broken, our hopes are depleted, our closest friend is darkness. And we also need

---

[8] Brueggemann and Bellinger, *Psalms*, 206.

those on the other side of lament who are willing to work on our behalf or be present in our pain.

These are important aspects of worship: Grief. Lament. Petition. Demand. Uncertainty. Struggle. Hope. Participation. They should be included and never avoided.

I offer one final thought as we transition to the next chapter. It's a confession that is pretty embarrassing, but I doubt it's all that unique: I feel like I'm just learning how to lament. It's not a natural or engrained prayer that is part of my regular routine. It *should be* because, as we can clearly see, lament is necessary. But for me, lament is still a *response*, it is a break from the normal, when the headlines get too loud or when the people in my congregation suffer tragedies that I haven't experienced myself and that I might not always fully understand. For this lack, I'm thankful that there are witnesses—consistent, powerful witnesses, who don't need to read an essay by Walter Brueggemann to be convinced of the benefits of lament.

At the outset, I admitted that in the midst of the barrage of truly lamentable situations, I struggle to find my own words. In addition to reciting the Hebrew Bible's time-honored prayers of lament, I would also do well to listen to the laments that are *already* being offered all around me. At times, the listening will entail extremely raw and difficult requests such as we find in the imprecatory psalms.

CHAPTER TWELVE

Did People Really Pray for *That* to Happen?

When I was writing my dissertation, I ran into another local pastor in a coffee shop. Seeing my books spread all over the place and knowing I was finishing up my degree, he bravely asked the question you should *never* ask a PhD student, "What's your dissertation about?" I kept it simple and told him I was writing on the ethics of Psalms. He replied, "The ethics of Psalms, huh? What is it? I mean, other than smashing the heads of your enemies' children against the rocks."

He was referring to Psalm 137, and its ... what should we say ... troubling, last line:

> Happy shall they be who take your little ones
>   and dash them against the rock! (v. 9)

The Imprecatory Psalms

Despite my initial frustration at the question, it's valid: what are the ethics of Psalms and, more to the point, what in the world do we do with Psalm 137? It's an imprecatory psalm—a sub-genre of lament that challenges God to deal with the pray-er's enemies, often in overtly violent ways. In the poetry of imprecation, heads are crushed, teeth are smashed, arms are broken, blood flows, pain is inflicted, and God is the *anticipated* agent in all of this hoped-for violence.

Like the lament psalms more generally, prayers asking God for some Tony Soprano–style protection are not infrequent. If my pastor friend hadn't cited Psalm 137, he could have just as easily used Psalm 58, which demands,

> O God, break the teeth in their mouths;
>> tear out the fangs of the young lions, O LORD!
> Let them vanish like water that runs away;
>> like grass let them be trodden down and wither.
> Let them be like the snail that dissolves into slime;
>> like the untimely birth that never sees the sun.
> Sooner than your pots can feel the heat of thorns,
>> whether green or ablaze, may he sweep them away!
> The righteous will rejoice when they see vengeance done;
>> they will bathe their feet in the blood of the wicked.
> People will say, "Surely there is a reward for the righteous;
>> surely there is a God who judges on earth." (vv. 6–11)

Or Psalm 69,

> Let their table be a trap for them,
>> a snare for their allies.
> Let their eyes be darkened so that they cannot see,
>> and make their loins tremble continually.
> Pour out your indignation upon them,
>> and let your burning anger overtake them.
> May their camp be a desolation;
>> let no one live in their tents.
> For they persecute those whom you have struck down,
>> and those whom you have wounded, they attack still more.
> Add guilt to their guilt;
>> may they have no acquittal from you.

Let them be blotted out of the book of the living;
    let them not be enrolled among the righteous.
But I am lowly and in pain;
    let your salvation, O God, protect me. (vv. 22–29)

Or Psalm 94,

O LORD, you God of vengeance,
    you God of vengeance, shine forth!
Rise up, O judge of the earth;
    give to the proud what they deserve!
…
But the LORD has become my stronghold,
    and my God the rock of my refuge.
He will repay them for their iniquity
    and wipe them out for their wickedness;
the LORD our God will wipe them out. (vv. 1–2, 22–23)

Or Psalm 139,

O that you would kill the wicked, O God,
    and that the bloodthirsty would depart from me—
those who speak of you maliciously,
    and lift themselves up against you for evil!
Do I not hate those who hate you, O LORD?
    And do I not loathe those who rise up against you?
I hate them with perfect hatred;
    I count them my enemies. (vv. 19–22)

These prayers are intense and extremely graphic, and as a result, many modern Western readers don't know what to do with them. For those seeking to pray these lines along with their ancient writers, the words of Jesus present a pretty significant source of tension. According to the biblical witness, when he taught his followers to pray, he failed to include anything about bathing their feet in the blood of their enemies. Quite the opposite, actually. Listeners were told to turn the other cheek when they got struck.

The discrepancy led our dear friend, Hermann Gunkel, to conclude, "It is utterly impossible for us to use the entire Psalter in Christian worship although earlier times may have so used it. The modern mind has found in it so much that is alien and even repellent that we have long been compelled to make selections for use in school and church and home."[1]

In 1974, the editors of the Catholic Church's revised Liturgy of the Hours reached a similar conclusion, removing three imprecatory psalms entirely (Pss 58, 83, and 109) and sections from twenty-two other psalms from the daily prayer resource.[2] The removal of "troubling" lines from the imprecatory prayers might save participants in worship from the cognitive dissonance of comparing the psalmists' requests for divine violence and Jesus's teaching in the Gospels. Even more pragmatically, their omission helps to alleviate God from receiving (even more) bad PR. Reading the imprecatory psalms' violent imagery in public worship could lend credence to the view that the people depicted in the pages of the Hebrew Bible are incomprehensible to us and their God is, too.

Removal is not a new approach. It was exemplified in the work of the early second century CE heretic named Marcion. He argued that the God of the Hebrew Bible and the depiction of Jesus in the Christian New Testament could not be reconciled. One was violent, the other was a pacifist. One laid down some pretty intense consequences for breaking laws, the other forgave his enemies and submitted himself

---

[1] Hermann Gunkel, "The Religion of the Psalms" in *Water for a Thirsty Land: Israelite Literature and Religion* (Minneapolis: Fortress Press, 2001). 134–67 (160).

[2] For a complete list see Gabriel Torretta, O.P., "Rediscovering the Imprecatory Psalms: A Thomistic Approach," *The Thomist* 80 (2016): 23–48.

to an undeserved death. These surface level disparities led Marcion to remove the God of the Hebrew Bible.

Marcion's views were rejected, but I bet there are those among us who can sympathize with his discomfort at some of the descriptions of a violent God in the Bible. Examples usually include Noah and the Flood, Abraham's near sacrifice of Isaac, the death of the Egyptians in plague narratives, the Passover, and the Red Sea crossing in Exodus, and Israel's conquest of the Promised Land, to name just a few. And yes, to this list, we could add the imprecatory psalms. When these prayers come up, readers might apologize for their existence and for the ancient people who read them and prayed them.

I wonder if such a defensive posture toward the imprecatory psalms says something. Here's what I mean: it's relatively easy to get on board with *lament*. It's good to hold God to task. It's good to ask for vindication. It's good to pray for divine involvement. It's good to acknowledge the wrong in the world. But imprecation? Asking God to break some teeth? Yeesh. Like the editors of the Liturgy of the Hours, it's much easier to conclude, "Nothing to see here! Keep moving! These prayers are just ancient people thinking ancient things! Let's skip them."

But does this response imply that some modern readers might not *need* imprecation? I think so. In fact, it's quite possible that many readers find themselves in the opposite position of a psalmist begging for divine intervention and justice. They don't need to be delivered from flesh and blood *enemies*. (What "enemies"? "You mean the people I unfollowed on Facebook?") And if they did, their station in life might allow them to take care of it themselves in a more "civilized" manner—a coffee meeting, a conversation, professional mediation. It's difficult for people of privilege and means to understand the need and the desperation and even the situations underlying imprecation. And as a result, the violent images included become problematic and embarrassing. It's easiest just to remove them entirely.

Here's my contention: one's level of discomfort with the imprecatory psalms is directly proportional to their *lack of need* for imprecation. For those who are oppressed, for those who have real enemies threatening them, the words of these psalms are much more relatable.

Maybe It's Not So Weird After All

Hebrew Bible scholar Erich Zenger observed a tendency in some readers (e.g., the non-oppressed) to ask about imprecation in terms of "can" and "should": *Can* we pray these psalms? *Should* we pray these psalms? Or is it better to go ahead and exclude them as remnants of our tradition's barbaric and violent past?[3] He goes on to note, the degree to which people are suffering, both in the context of the psalms and in the context of its modern-day readers, is not usually taken into account. If either would be seen in light of their oppression or abuse, Zenger implies, our answer to the can/should question would be different.

For an exilic community in the sixth century BCE, for instance, Psalm 137 was not problematic. At all. In fact, it was deeply meaningful. The trauma involved in the loss of their home, the loss of their children, the forced migration from their land (which, remember, was promised to them by God), the destruction of their center of worship (which was believed to house the very presence of God) is extreme. It's no wonder they prayed for vengeance in such overt terms. The psalmist's words represent a raw and honest request for God to execute justice. We may struggle to understand because of how far removed we are from this context.

Interestingly, many US Christians incorporated Psalm 137 in their public worship soon after 9/11. Apparently, when oppression is communal and close to home—and no longer "over there" somewhere or relegated to the past—it's easier to find ourselves in texts that may have been avoided at one point due to their perceived difficulties. To be clear,

---

[3] Erich Zenger, *A God of Vengeance?: Understanding the Psalms of Divine Wrath*, trans. Linda M. Maloney (Louisville: Westminster John Knox Press, 1996). See especially pages 1–23.

I'm not advocating for more Sunday sermons on Psalm 137 necessarily. I only want to suggest that there was a moment when what was previously incomprehensible (the imprecatory psalms) spoke directly to the feelings and emotions of a growing number of people, who could root its language in their own experience. After waging a twenty-year war against "terror," the *collective* US point of reference with suffering has certainly diminished, and many (non-oppressed American) readers have returned to theorizing, forgetful that there was a time when their desire was for vengeance.

In his wonderful and poignant book *Reading While Black*, Esau McCaulley observes the imprecatory psalms "are words of a people who know *rage*, a people who know what it is like to turn to those with power hoping for recompense only to be pushed further into the mud. These are the words of those who walk past homes and families living in luxury knowing that this wealth is bought with the price of their suffering. The oppressor's children live at ease while children of the oppressed starve."[4] These words echo those of famed black activist and author, James Baldwin, spoken in 1961 during the height of the US civil rights movement:

> To be a Negro in this country and to be relatively conscious is to be in a state of rage almost, almost all of the time—and in one's work. And part of the rage is this: It isn't only what is happening to you. But it's what's happening all around you and all of the time in the face of the most extraordinary and criminal indifference, indifference of most white people in this country, and their ignorance. Now, since this is so, it's a great temptation to simplify the issues under the illusion that if you simplify them enough, people will recognize them. I think this illusion is very dangerous because, in fact, it isn't the way it works. A complex

---

[4] Esau McCaulley, *Reading While Black: African American Biblical Interpretation as an Exercise in Hope* (Downers Grove, IL: IVP Academic, 2020), 123.

thing can't be made simple. You simply have to try to deal with it in all its complexity and hope to get that complexity across.[5]

In other words, there is a continued need for the imprecatory psalms, which means, before we seek to remove them from the Psalter and from communal worship, we need to appreciate the context of these prayers, and acknowledge the injustices and oppressions that were faced by the exiled Israelites are still very much present in our world today.

Are You Saying It's OK to Ask God to Kill Babies?

No, definitely not. I don't think that particular tidbit from the ancient world has a lot of crossover with our context today. But I *am* saying it's OK to present an honest and emotion-filled request to God in prayer. As Fr Richard Rohr would say, everything belongs.[6] Whatever rage one feels, whatever desperate requests one makes, God can handle it, even if we say things that seem to go against our guiding ethical principles.

For those with lived experiences of oppression, the inclusion of the imprecatory psalms (and our continued use of them) bears witness to the many voices in the past that have raged against injustice and demanded that God respond. For those who have not experienced oppression, these very same psalms are an important reminder that injustice exists and persists. And more than mere acknowledgment, the imprecatory psalms extend an invitation to raise one's voice in pursuit of justice on behalf of those who cannot advocate for themselves and amplify the voices of those who can.

---

[5] To listen to the full conversation, which originally aired in 1961 on WBAI-FM under the title "The Negro in American Culture," visit https://www.youtube.com/watch?v=jNpitdJSXWY
[6] See Richard Rohr, *Everything Belongs: The Gift of Contemplative Prayer*, rev. ed. (New York: The Crossroad Publishing Company, 2003).

I need this reminder. I'm a middle-class white guy, writing these words in a fancy coffee shop, sipping an oat milk cortado, listening to "Sob Rock" by John Mayer. What do I know about suffering? What do I know about the need for imprecation? Honestly, it's just as important for me to consider whether people need to offer imprecations *because of me*—and my privilege and my biases and my participation in (and benefitting from) oppressive systems of injustice.

The last thing I want to do here is democratize Baldwin's words, as if all of our experiences are equivalent. They aren't. But I will admit, that if anyone is relatively conscious (myself included), we *should be* in a state of rage over the oppression, mistreatment, abuse, prejudice, and bigotry that is all around us ... because it *is* all around us. I should heed the invitation of the imprecatory psalms and call God to tear down the lofty on behalf of the oppressed. And I should honestly assess if "the lofty" is describing me.

I know this seems to fly in the face of the teachings of Jesus. It also seems to fly in the face of my adopted ethic of non-violence. (I think the next section will help a little bit on these important issues, so sit tight.) At present, I want to be clear: I'm *only* arguing that if Psalms teaches us anything, it's that honesty is good and the reality of injustice should evoke an emotional outpouring. I'd also add that we should do our best Brené Brown impression and hear the psalmists' pleas with some empathy. In a psalm like Psalm 137, these ancient people have lost everything. They are suffering. Their prayers reflect that, and if we allow ourselves to see it, their words make more sense given the situation.

The God of Vengeance

The pray-er in Psalm 137, though bold and expressive and frighteningly intense, is actually *relinquishing* their desire for vengeance—as well as any plan they might have to inflict violence—over to God. They are asking, in no uncertain terms, that the *God of justice* execute justice.

The exiles envisioned in Psalm 137 didn't "storm the castle." Those who lost family members to the Babylonian superpower didn't pick up implements of war. They didn't call on the military to start marching.

They petitioned God to respond.

This is, in effect, God's people saying, "Here's where I am, God. Here's what I want. Here's how I'm processing my grief, and it's probably not really healthy. I need you to take it, God, and do something just." Sadly, this is not representative of how Psalm 137 was used post-9/11. More often than not, it seems the people who preached it wanted to justify their enactments of vengeance. They wanted to take it into their own hands. In their reading (and preaching), the cries of the psalmist became less of a relinquishing and more of a call to arms, as if a violent outburst is what God wanted. But that completely misses the clarifying call of Jesus—a call to peace, a call to non-violence, a call to turning our cheek once it is struck and praying for our enemies and those who persecute us. His is a call to entrust the God of justice to be just.

The psalmist's honest plea is actually, in a weird way, a beautiful act of trust. We can miss this important reality about imprecation due to our preoccupation with the hypothetical *should we/can we* pray like this question. We get overly focused on the psalms' inclusion of violence, while failing to see the psalmists' relinquishing of violence. Questions like the above miss the point, and when we ask them, we diminish the psalmists' (and maybe our own) very real human emotion and need in the face of injustice. And in the same turn, we diminish any hope that *God* will enact justice.

CHAPTER THIRTEEN

In Psalms, God Is a Warrior & That's OK

Here's a theme that has been lurking just underneath the surface of this entire book: the gap between the cultural context of the ancient audience(s) of Psalms and that of the modern reader is pretty substantial. It appeared yet again in the last chapter as we discussed the psalmists' entreaties that God enact violence on their enemies/oppressors/dominant world powers. It doesn't even matter if God ever responded positively to these requests or not. The communal belief that *God would want to* puts many modern readers in unfamiliar and uncomfortable territory.

Divine violence is a big problem. The oddity of the Hebrew Bible's witness to God's taming primordial chaos by crushing the heads of mythical sea dragons is one thing. Depictions of enacted divine violence on human beings—not just *wishing* or *praying* for an enactment of divine violence, as in the imprecatory psalms—but celebrations of what are believed to be *actual* examples of divine violence against *actual* human beings is another thing altogether. And that is exactly what some of the poetic images in Psalms give us: celebrations of a violent God, who went to war for Israel.

This is not a new problem and, as a result, a lot of really good work has already been done on the ancient Near Eastern background informing the stories of divine violence in the Hebrew Bible. One of the clear takeaways is the importance of beginning with the admission that these are, in fact, *ancient* stories. That reality doesn't alleviate all of the interpretive issues, but it's helpful to acknowledge. What troubles us now probably didn't trouble ancient readers. In their world, the expectation was gods went to war, and the good ones were victorious. In some ways, the biblical text is simply playing into that cultural expectation, which shouldn't be surprising. Its authors were not 21st-century non-violent activists.

Many of the studies on divine violence have added an additional perspective that some readers find helpful, namely, the historical perspective. A general line in mainstream biblical scholarship is that some of the most notorious stories of divine violence didn't *really* happen— either not at all or not in the ways they are described in the Bible. This includes the Flood story, the plagues and the Red Sea crossing in the exodus narratives, and the stories of Israel's genocidal "conquest" under Joshua's leadership. On one level, historical challenges help to alleviate *some* of the issues. If, for instance, these stories didn't happen as they are portrayed in the Bible, then readers are afforded some breathing room because God is taken off the hook. No real, enacted violence, no problem. Ehh ... sort of. I'll come back to this.

First, for folks who haven't read much behind-the-scenes Hebrew Bible scholarship, let me briefly explain how and why scholars began to doubt the historicity of these stories to begin with.

Joshua 6 is a good place to start. It tells the famous Sunday school story of "Joshua and the battle of Jericho." To recap, the Israelites are instructed to begin their conquest of the Promised Land in miraculous fashion. Led by the Ark of the Covenant (a sacred box that symbolized the very presence of God), the people are commanded to march around the Canaanite city of Jericho once a day for six straight days, and then seven times on the seventh consecutive day. At the end of their seventh lap on the seventh day, the priests would blow their horns and the people would shout, and, apparently, that would cause the walls of the city to fall down. So this is exactly what they do, and that is exactly what happens. When the walls crumble on the seventh day, the extermination of the city's inhabitants (minus Rahab and her family; see Joshua 2) takes place. Excellent. It's a great kids' story. (I'm joking.)

When the details of Joshua 6 were compared to the discovered physical remains of Jericho, historical problems emerged. So much so that the overwhelming majority of archaeologists and biblical scholars contend Jericho would have been a virtually uninhabited, unwalled city during the time frame that a Joshua figure would have been leading a band of Israelites into the Promised Land. In other words, based on what archaeologists unearthed, most scholars conclude the biblical story couldn't possibly have happened in the exact way the text states— no one and no standing walls would have been there! To be fair, there is a small contingent of scholars, most of whom are evangelicals, who challenge these findings. I don't mean to disparage their work, but it seems that their conclusions are based primarily on their view of the Bible (and what it must be) rather than a fair reading of the archaeological evidence. We can debate that another day. Here's the point: if the majority position is granted, it saves perplexed readers from having to explain the deaths of an entire city. Since no one lived there, God didn't *really* kill anyone.

Whatever relief one might experience by this proposal, however, should be quickly tempered. The stories of Israel's complete decimation (sort of)[1] of Jericho and the other cities of Canaan are still *in the Bible.* Even if these troubling events didn't happen in the way they are presented, there were still a bunch of ancients *wishing* they did and telling stories and singing songs *as if* they did. The understanding of God, at this time, included God's warrior status, and that's a problem for us.[2]

---

[1] I say "sort of" because the biblical text argues with itself over the presentation of the conquest. In some passages, "everyone" was killed (see Deuteronomy 9, Joshua 11), and in others, "some people still remained" (see, for example, Exodus 23, Joshua 13 and 23, and Judges 2). The historicity of these stories, then, is not just an archaeological issue: it's a textual one, too. Unpacking the web of issues is beyond the scope of this study ... and the point I'm trying to make.

[2] We've talked about the development of ideas within the Hebrew Bible. It's important not to apply a broad brush to the entire Hebrew Bible corpus on something like God's "warrior status."

The interpretive situation is roughly the same for the exodus event. The historicity of the plagues and Israel's departure from Egyptian servitude and the Red Sea crossing as well as Israel's eventual wilderness wandering is questioned on a number of grounds—textual, logical, chronological, and archaeological. On the actual exodus of a group of pre-Israelite slaves from Egyptian oppression, scholars seem content to say "something may have happened … but it definitely wasn't on the size and scope of what the Bible portrays." (The plagues are more mythical in nature. It is a war between "the gods.") But, again, regardless of the degree to which we view the stories in Exodus as accurate depictions of real, historical events, they are *still in the Bible*. To put it another way, *in our sacred texts*, God is said to end the lives of an entire country's population of firstborn male children and drown an entire army in the Red Sea. The stories in Exodus are overly focused on this point—it is *God* who did this. The book reiterates in numerous ways Yahweh's role in the warfare against Egypt. As Moses encourages the people, "The LORD will fight for you, and you have only to keep still" (Exod 14:14).[3]

The historicity of the Flood narrative is also rejected by the overwhelming majority of biblical scholars. It appears to be Israel's version of a well-known trope about water events in the ancient world. There may have been some historical event (some flooding) that originally caused ancient people to create these stories, but it seems pretty clear that they aren't meant to be read literally or historically, as if there were a real Noah figure who built a big boat and loaded it with a bunch of cute animals. But still, even if its questionable historical status is accepted, it only helps us so much. This story of mass *divine* extermination is still *in the Bible*.

---

[3] Pete Enns has a great line about the last phrase (which can also read "you have only to keep quiet") in his Exodus commentary. He writes, "This is not … a word of comfort …. Rather, this is a terse, impatient command on Moses' part. In Hebrew, the last part of the verse is a mere two Hebrew words, which are best translated as 'You be quiet!' or 'Shut up!'" See Peter Enns, *Exodus* (The NIV Application Commentary; Grand Rapids, MI: Zondervan, 2000), 273.

Divine violence was part of the cultural milieu informing the authors of the Bible. It was not problematic *for them*. It was part of their world.

The Psalms and a Violent God

Psalms contributes to this discussion in that it taps into the ancient imagination by celebrating a warring God. Psalm 98, for example, says,

> O sing to the LORD a new song,
>   for he has done marvelous things.
> His right hand and his holy arm
>   have gotten him victory.
> The LORD has made known his victory;
>   he has revealed his vindication in the sight of the nations.
> He has remembered his steadfast love *(hesed)* and faithfulness
>   to the house of Israel.
> All the ends of the earth have seen
>   the victory of our God. (vv. 1–3)

As commentators note, this poem has a lot in common with the Song of the Sea in Exodus 15, which was offered after the Red Sea crossing. Both texts celebrate the military victories of God and feature them as the basis for praise—because God defeated Israel's enemies (the Egyptians), readers should offer praise. In fact, the psalm expresses an intended universal reach. *All the earth* is called to praise on the basis of God's military might. And it's not just people. It's all of creation—the seas, the floods, the hills—they will all participate in praise because Israel's God is a warrior.

To limit the scope of the psalm's inference to God's demonstration of power against Egypt, though, is to misread it. In Israel's mind, God demonstrated military might against Egypt *and* in the conquest *and* in

Israel's battles against world powers *and* any other time they went to war and won.

Some have postulated that the content of Psalm 98 suggests its use in corporate celebrations welcoming Israel's army home from a successful battle. Who knows? The singing of Psalm 98 does show the people's theological cards. God did this. The victory therefore belongs to God, not the ones swinging the sword. For the psalmist, and for their audience, God was a warrior and when God won, everyone—the whole world—should turn and praise.

A Bottom-Up Approach

In my line of work, I have fielded many variants on the question of divine violence in the Hebrew Bible. Every pastor has, I'm sure. Rarely are these questions focused on Psalms, but if they were, my approach would be the same.

First, I would affirm the problem: God's depiction as a warrior is difficult. Honestly, it can't be defended. Richard Dawkins and the New Atheists have every right to claim these stories are based on a barbaric image of a bloodthirsty tyrant.[4] And when ancient people praised their God for it? That's barbaric too. When we reduce the issue to trite explanations like, "God can do whatever God wants" or "Since God did it, those people must have deserved it," it doesn't help.

I think arguments like the ones offered by the New Atheists lack nuance, but on the surface, I get it. Flooding the entire world or killing

---

[4] Dawkins, we should note, is working from the assumption that these stories didn't happen in history, so that "defense" will not prove helpful. In fact, on the issue of the conquest narrative, he writes, "The point is that, whether true or not, the Bible is held up to us as the source of our morality. And the Bible story of Joshua's destruction of Jericho, and the invasion of the Promised Land, in general, is morally indistinguishable from Hitler's invasion of Poland, or Saddam Hussein's massacres of the Kurds and the Marsh Arabs." See Richard Dawkins, *The God Delusion* (New York: Mariner Books, 2008), 280.

the firstborn male children of the Egyptians or drowning their army in the Red Sea or commanding Joshua to kill everything that breathes is not a good look for the object of our worship. (Our defense of it isn't either!) If I thought it was a description of who God *actually* is, I would struggle too.

Second, I remind folks that these texts—the exodus event, the conquest, Psalm 98—offer culturally-embedded snapshots of who God was believed to be at that time. One of the reasons it doesn't translate as easily is due, yet again, to the cultural gap between ancient Israel and our contemporary context. That said, I don't want to insinuate that the problem is *solely* due to our diverse cultural contexts. Jesus's non-violent ethic creates significant issues for us, too. There appears to be a good deal of movement from the culturally-embedded snapshot offered in some parts of the Hebrew Bible and in the teachings of Jesus. But even with this movement, it's important to admit that we shouldn't expect the Bible (even Jesus) to adopt or observe *our* cultural mores. It's an ancient text through and through. It speaks in ancient ways to ancient audiences. When we read the Bible, we are confronting and engaging a completely foreign cultural context.

Third, part of that operative cultural context in the world of the Hebrew Bible was that gods functioned as warriors in their religious context. No one would have batted an eye at the stories of divine violence because that's what they thought gods did. As such, the psalmists participated in and wrote from the standpoint of the dominant cultural milieu. That's why we get texts that describe God as a warrior and romanticized depictions of divine violence.

Fourth, we need to ask why we would expect anything different from an ancient text. The Bible, all of it, is set within specific context(s), and it was written in ways its audience would have understood. When we expect the Bible to transcend its culture (and end up in ours!), I think we set ourselves up for some bad readings. All of the stuff we have talked about in this section was embedded within a culture. And if we are to understand the theological concepts, we need to understand the beliefs, expectations, society, and language of that context. It's hard work. It's not impossible, but it's not as easy as just reading the words on the page and judging them based on where we are.

Fifth, all of the foregoing leads me to believe that what we have in Psalm 98 is best described as a "bottom-up" understanding of God. Psalm 98 is a culturally-embedded snapshot written from the standpoint of the psalmist to describe who they believed God was. It is not necessarily an accurate representation of who God is *ontologically* (in God's very being). For Christian readers, the image of Jesus, who is claimed to be the exact representation of God, challenges the view that God is *actually* a warrior in the way the authors of the Hebrew Bible think. Jesus was different. His ethic was different. There's a contradiction between Jesus and the depiction of God in the Hebrew Bible. It's lessened if we read something like Psalm 98 as a depiction of God from the bottom-up, that is, from the standpoint of an ancient people who believed gods fought for their people. In their mind, when they went to war, God went with them, went before them, won their battles, was a warrior. So that's how they described God in their poems and prayers.

But I'd argue that God wasn't *actually* violent in the old days and then became less violent over time as society changed. I'd say the images we have are due to the fact that the ancients believed God fought their battles. Many Christians today, for various reasons (Jesus being one of them), believe that God is not at the head of any battles. Both interpretive groups, the ancients putting the Hebrew Bible together and Christians today, are doing their best to understand God in light of their contexts. All projections of who God is are culturally-embedded and cannot capture God for all time. I don't have it all figured out. And neither did the psalmists. For them, God was a warrior. For me, God isn't, at least not in a "when we go fight a war on terror, God kills 'the bad guys' for us" sort of way. Both conclusions, mine and the psalmists, are incomplete because describing an infinite God is hard work!

Uhhh ...

Some of you might have read point five above and said, "Nope. That's definitely wrong." That's OK. I know it feels like a leap. I certainly didn't get there after reading a few paragraphs in a book by some guy I don't know. Hopefully where we can agree is in saying Psalms sometimes presents God as a violent warrior and even if that image made sense to its ancient readers, it makes less sense to some readers today in light of Jesus.

However we choose to traverse the cultural gap from then to now, from Israel to wherever we are, that's the task ahead of us. And it's a task we shouldn't take lightly or for granted. By engaging in this work, we join millennia of Jewish and Christian reading communities who have wrestled with images of God that are troubling. You could say that Jesus and the New Testament authors provide us with a glimpse of this work. Jesus was well-versed in the images of the divine warrior, and yet he favored non-violence in his "warfare" against evil, sin, and death. His example provides an important counter-testimony to the ways victories were believed to be won in the Hebrew Bible.

When we read the Psalms, we must confront its "oldness," its embeddedness, its culturally-derived images of the divine. And then we need to make sense of these characteristics. It's difficult, but it's also important and potentially life-giving. If that's too big of a reach, this work will at least lead to an honest and nuanced starting point for a good reading of Psalms.

CHAPTER FOURTEEN

Lessons in Being Subversive

The overwhelming focus of Psalms is on God, whether its compositions are praising God for past actions—past deliverances, past demonstrations of *hesed*, past military victories—or whether they are petitioning God to deliver—to act on behalf of the poor and oppressed, to vindicate and defend them against the ungodly, to war against injustice or flesh-and-blood enemies. The book is relentlessly theological.

But the divine is not the only focus in Psalms. The king is addressed as well. Ethically, there was an expectation that the king would model divine characteristics—to rule with justice and equity (like God does), to advocate for and protect the poor and oppressed (like God does), to oppose injustice in its many forms (like God does), to demonstrate faithfulness (like God does). In fact, the king was believed to function as God's "vice-regent" or "vicegerent" or "viceroy," all fancy nerd words meaning the king was divinely established and expected to rule *for* God *over* God's people *in* God's stead.[1] As a result, more than a few prayers

---

[1] Much of our attention has focused on the exilic or post-exilic setting of the Psalms. Prayers for the king, though, clearly depend upon a setting when kings ruled! Dating psalms is always tricky business, but such an overt clue allows us to view prayers for the king as a potentially early witness to Israel's worship.

in Psalms specify the role of the king and hold him accountable to keep his end of the bargain.

Worryingly Ideological or Wonderfully Devious

In this chapter, we will look at one example, Psalm 72. Not only is this poem one of the clearest prayers for Israel's king, it also showcases what prayers for the king *did*. I'll go ahead and spoil it for you: prayers for the king set a frighteningly high standard. In fact, these prayers could be read as subversive acts of worship offered on behalf of the pray-ers to ensure their protection by the king. Interestingly, in Psalm 72, the only "unequivocal prayer"—the only direct request to God on behalf of the king—comes in the opening verse:[2]

> Give the king your justice, O God,
> > and your righteousness to a king's son. (v. 1)

The rest of the psalm focuses on the results that will follow not *if*, but *when*, the king is successful in enacting God's justice and righteousness. This is probably lost on most readers due to the translation of the prayer. It renders the verbs following verse 1 as a hope, implying that the verbs are part of the pray-er's continued list of requests to God: "may the king …" do this or that. Another way to read those lines, however, is as a collection of affirmative statements: "The king will …" do this or that. Read in this way, the psalmist states that once the king is granted God's justice and righteousness:

> He *will* judge your people with righteousness,
> > and your poor with justice.
> The mountains *will* yield prosperity for the people,

---

[2] John Goldingay, *Psalms 42–89* (Baker Commentary on the Old Testament Wisdom and Psalms; Grand Rapids, MI: Baker Academic, 2007), 381.

and the hills, in righteousness.
He *will* defend the cause of the poor of the people,
    give deliverance to the needy,
    and crush the oppressor.
He *will* live while the sun endures,
    and as long as the moon, throughout all generations.
He *will* be like rain that falls on the mown grass,
    like showers that water the earth.
In his days righteousness *will* flourish
    and peace abound, until the moon is no more. (vv. 2–7)

When you consider who is offering the prayer (i.e., not the king!), it is sort of hilarious in its overt subversion. It's like a mom in the principal's office saying what her child will and won't do in the future. "Oh, don't worry, ma'am. Going forward, my child *will* behave. You *will not* have to see them again." Read in this way, the prayer for the king is less a petition and more an extremely loaded statement of fact. The king *will* rule on behalf of the poor and the oppressed. And when he does, he *will* be blessed. The pray-ers are stacking the deck in their favor; they are the potential recipients of the king's judicious rule.

As the poem unfolds line by line, you can imagine the king beginning to feel the weight as his responsibilities pile up. But to sweeten the deal, it states that protection and care for the weak (read: for the pray-ers) will lead to the king's renown. The pray-ers' hope for equity, in other words, is incentivized. As such, their requests are mutually beneficial: you do good to us, king, and you'll get good for yourself and your kingdom. In fact, if the king lives up to his end of the bargain, the pray-er goes on, "All kings fall down before him, all nations give him service" (v. 11). This is specifically *because of* his righteous and just treatment of the poor and needy.

Goldingay rightly describes the prayer as "worryingly ideological or wonderfully devious."[3] It's ideological because, on the one hand,

---

[3] Goldingay, *Psalms 42–89*, 393.

the prayer affirms the political institution. The king is the one with authority. The king is in charge. That is not questioned. The institution will continue to stand. But it is devious because the people hold the king's feet to the fire. If the king wants acclaim and power, he must implement an equitable rule, which will be to the people's great benefit. Clearly, there is tension here.

The prayer for the king in Psalm 72 was not primarily to/for God—that's just the first line—nor was it primarily to/for the king, as if the pray-ers were motivated by an altruistic concern for the king's personal blessings. The prayer was, perhaps fundamentally so, to/for the community, with an invocation to the divine to really seal the deal. "Do this, king, and we'll get what we want. I mean, you will too, but that's not important right now. This one is for us. Oh, and remember, God is listening."

Of Solomon

Another way to approach the psalm is suggested by its title. Psalm 72 is a psalm "of/to/for/on behalf of/inspired by/concerning/about/dedicated to/belonging *to Solomon.*" Whether you agree with my assessment about the timing of the psalm titles (they were late additions) or their interpretation (they don't indicate authorship), think about this: because of the title, the psalm's subversive prayer for Israel's king is forever linked with Solomon. If ever there was a poster child for the complete opposite of what this prayer is after—for *inequity*, for *not protecting* the poor and oppressed—it's Solomon! The stories of his life prove that. He may have been depicted as wise, but his many building projects and high tax rates put a "heavy yoke" on the people (see 1 Kings 12:1–9). This later editorial addition, then, functions as a subtle reminder that Solomon, and every other human king, really, failed to live up to the high bar set by the psalm. It may also be a reminder that these prayers don't necessarily "work."

One more time … remember the judgment of Ezekiel 34 on the state of kingship? (See Chapter Two.) It compares kings to bad shepherds. In fact, the author argues that Israel's and Judah's kings/shepherds led to the demise of their respective kingdoms. The kings were shepherds "feeding themselves" (v. 2). They didn't strengthen the weak. They didn't heal the sick. They didn't bind up the injured. They didn't seek the lost. They didn't do what Psalm 72 demands. Instead, they ruled the people "with force and harshness" (v. 4). Despite a few good examples, the kings didn't manifest a god-like rule. They failed as God's vice-regents.

This historical reality has led some commentators to wonder if Psalm 72 functioned as "liturgical cover" for the king. The psalm offers the right words, it describes what the kings *should have done*, but it doesn't reflect the real intent of the king to *actually* care for the poor. It's the type of stuff that is said in worship to give the people hope, or, viewed through a political lens, it's like promises made on the campaign trail—they detail what a candidate will do if elected, but don't eventuate once the elected official is in office.

It's hard to say if this reading of the psalm is correct. It requires way too much background knowledge that we just don't have. Did the king care about saying the right things? I'm inclined to say no. The psalm reads more like a hope-filled prayer of the people that the king *actually* be equitable and good. According to the biblical presentation of the kings, it would have been a necessity.

Whatever the case, "Psalm 72 still challenges rulers to heed its call: that authority is only valid when based on care for the poor; that the humblest have first claim on state resources of power and money; that unless they defend the oppressed and repress the oppressor, they have no claim to any of the privileges that go with authority."[4] And even if the prayer was subversive, the sad reality is, the kings didn't live up to the call.

---

[4] Walter Houston, "The King's Preferential Option for the Poor: Rhetoric, Ideology and Ethics in Psalm 72," *Biblical Interpretation* 7 (1999): 362.

CHAPTER FIFTEEN

Humanity in Psalms: Somewhere Between Gods & Worms

Remember, my goal in this book is to expose just a few of the culturally-embedded theological snapshots in Psalms. That's an important
disclaimer as we begin to unpack its views on humanity, which are (1)
still very much culturally-embedded, (2) not uniform, and (3) not a
large point of emphasis in the collection. The first and second quali-
fiers should be expected at this point. Psalmists bring many different
ideas to bear in their poetic compositions. They reflect their cultural
moment and, when taken together, they produce a diverse conglom-
eration of teaching. Psalms' views on humanity are no exception. The
third qualifier should also be familiar by now. The book of Psalms is
relentlessly theological. Its compositions, even when they focus on
kings or humans, are about God above all else—who God is, what
God has done, what one can expect from God. Whatever readers learn
about humanity in Psalms is enveloped in a much more foundational
theological teaching. The psalmists, in other words, model what James
Luther Mays has so eloquently written, "We can say 'human being'
only after we have learned to say 'God.'"[1]

---

[1] James L. Mays, "What Is a Human Being? Reflections on Psalm 8" *Theology
Today* 50 (1993–94), 511–20 (519).

In this chapter, I'd like to juxtapose two of Psalms' "takes" on the nature of humanity: Psalms 51 and 8. More accurately, I'll compare a take that is *actually* in Psalms and another that has been regularly (and wrongly) inserted. I'll summarize the latter for you: humans are hopelessly sinful from birth. If you've attended a church that offers a weekly "altar call," you've probably heard some variation of this anthropological view. Because of its familiarity, I won't say too much about it here, nor will I attack the evangelistic aims of churches. I will, however, push against how many modern readers use and apply Psalm 51 in this way to support their beliefs and practices.

The other psalm, Psalm 8, offers a much healthier view of humanity. The psalmist's claims are surprisingly positive. We'll look at each, in turn.

Anthropological View #1: You and David and Everyone Else are Terrible People

Psalm 51 is one of the thirteen psalms with a "long title." Psalms' editors linked the poem with the infamous story of David's sexual assault and impregnation of Bathsheba and his consequent murder of her husband, Uriah (2 Sam 11–12). This identification with David, no doubt, was encouraged by the content of the poem, which is clearly confessional. The author of the psalm acknowledges their sin, albeit in vague and hyperbolic terms, and pleads God for forgiveness.[2] For the ancient

---

[2] Interestingly, the way Psalm 51 seeks to "acquire" divine forgiveness does not involve sacrifice, which is a common misconception about how forgiveness worked in the Hebrew Bible. The psalmist simply pleads God to forgive. Many readers tend to differentiate confession in the Hebrew Bible and in a Christian context—Christians can just ask; they don't have to offer sacrifices. But, at least in Psalm 51, there is little difference in a Christian understanding of forgiveness, which is attainable upon request, and that of the psalmist. The psalm implies when you sin, you plead for God's forgiveness, and expect God to grant it.

editors, the poem sounded like something David would do (or should have done) after his immoral conduct in the Bathsheba story, so they linked the two together for future readers.[3] The title, however, should not be read as a historical note. It is a "hermeneutical" linking of ideas: "Read this psalm of confession with David's sin in mind."

I bring this psalm up here, in a chapter on the Psalms' view of humanity, because there's a line in the poem that has become definitional for many communities' guiding anthropological beliefs. Sadly, as Rolf Jacobson claims, this line also happens to be "one of the most misinterpreted verses in the Psalter."[4] It reads, "Indeed, I was born guilty, a sinner when my mother conceived me" (Ps 51:5).

This verse is set within the psalmist's confession and serves as part of their plea for grace. The problem is the psalmist's personal admission is often wrongly interpreted as a universal, anthropological statement—one that proves the legitimacy of a theological idea called, "original sin." Jacobson describes original sin as "a depraved nature that is intrinsic to every human being, passed on to us by the first human pair."[5] In other words, "original sin" claims when Adam and Eve disobeyed in the Garden, their guilt/shame/sinfulness and its consequences were passed on to everyone else. What results is a theological/anthropological challenge to the notion that humans are born cute, plump, totally snuggable, little bundles of joy. Or if they happen to be cute and totally snuggable, they aren't innocent. Just like the psalmist, they are devious little sinners before they ever enter the world.

As I already noted, this sort of thinking underlines the way many churches explain "the gospel": because of Adam and Eve's sin in the Garden, we are sinners destined for God's wrath … so you better accept Jesus as your personal Lord and Savior or else you'll burn in

---

[3] There is also a verbal connection between Psalm 51:4 ("Against you, you alone, have I sinned") and David's confession in 2 Samuel 12:13 ("I have sinned against the LORD").

[4] deClaissé-Walford, Jacobson, and Tanner, *The Book of Psalms*, 456.

[5] Ibid.

Hell for all eternity! This version of the Christian gospel, as damaging as it may be, isn't based solely on Psalm 51. Paul seems to say a few things about "original sin" and a related concept that Calvinists call "total depravity" (i.e., humans are *completely* sinful and unable to be anything other without the Spirit's intervention). It goes beyond my point to engage Paul's culturally-embedded theology. I will note, however, that this reading of Paul is not the only view. In fact, in the texts that are usually cited in this discussion, Paul is motivated by the goal of *including Gentiles in the family of God*. He isn't writing a treatise on "how to get saved," complete with step-by-step instructions for an altar call. When we reduce Paul's work to "the Romans' Road," we are most likely missing the point, which for Paul is this: the gospel is not limited to Jewish Christians. When he says we are "all sinners" (Rom 3:23), he actually means, "both" are sinners—Jews and Gentiles.[6]

Regardless of how we choose to read Paul, taking *our* theological commitments and reading them back into the psalmist's poetry in Psalm 51 pushes the limits of the poem's clearly hyperbolic confession. It causes us to move much too quickly from the psalmist's exaggerated acknowledgment of *their* sin—"I was born guilty, a sinner when my mother conceived me"—to a purported declaration of some universal truth for all humanity—"We are all born guilty, sinners when our mothers conceived us." That wasn't the psalmist's point. Some commentators would say that this line of thought wasn't even conceivable in the world of the Hebrew Bible. "A more plausible interpretation ... is that the psalmist is expressing in these words the all-pervasive quality of guilt which accompanies the wrong-doing" ... *their* wrongdoing.[7] It was not meant to be a statement on the human condition *in utero*.

But it's preached this way, as an all-encompassing statement affecting all of us equally. And the damage has been incalculable.

---

[6] For a deeper dive into Paul's message in Romans—and the cultural, religious and political contexts in which Paul was writing—check out *Romans for Normal People* by J.R. Daniel Kirk (The Bible for Normal People, 2022).

[7] deClaissé-Walford, Jacobson, and Tanner, *The Book of Psalms*, 456.

Anthropological View #2: What is Humanity? Pretty Important, It Turns Out.

Psalm 8 tells a very different story about humanity. And this time, it's a story the psalmist is actually intending to tell.

Psalm 8 is technically a praise psalm—the first one in the book. But it's a bit weird, formally. Contrary to what we've come to expect from praise psalms, there is no call to praise, either at the beginning or end. Instead, the poem is framed by a powerful doxological statement.

> O LORD, our Sovereign [Lit: Yahweh, our Lord],
> how majestic is your name in all the earth! (vv. 1a and 9)

There are no stated reasons for praising in the poem either—no explicit motivations introduced by a "for/because" clause. Between the poem's *inclusio* in verses 1a and 9, the psalmist implicitly details why God's name is so majestic. It's because of God's creative activity, which is observable in the heavens, the moon, the stars, and the other works of God's hands. All of this provides evidence of God's majesty (vv. 3–4).

Many readers see clear parallels between Psalm 8 and Genesis 1, not only in the shared focus on God's creative work, but in the description of God's foes in the creative process as well—God's "enemy and avenger" (Psalm 8:2). As we have already explored, these terms probably refer to God's taming of primordial chaos.

The psalmist's praise of creation, however, is preparatory. It moves readers toward the center of the poem and the writer's related confusion concerning another created entity: humanity. God is majestic, and we see that in the works of God's hands, but …

> What are human beings that you are mindful of them,
> mortals that you care for them? (v. 4)

To steal an image from a friend, these are the kinds of existential questions we might ask "whenever we find ourselves lying with close friends on the hood of a Thunderbird staring up at the night sky."[8] Why does God care ... *about us?*

Note the parallelisms in verse 4—the word pair translated "human beings" and "mortals," and the thematically linked verbs "to be mindful" and "to care." Most commentators claim the distinction between the referents, human beings and mortals (lit: the sons of Adam), is negligible. But there is some important verbal dynamism that occurs when we move from one colon to the next. The first colon considers the divine's mindfulness of humanity. The second intensifies God's involvement. As Goldingay notes, "God thinks first, then acts."[9] Both actions are mind-boggling for the psalmist.

If a reader is approaching the poem with a pre-loaded Psalm 51 anthropology—humanity is tainted and broken and guilty—the psalmist's question is more than fair. But this reading-in poisons the well. Thankfully, the psalmist is immune to importing slanted Pauline theology. They go in a completely different direction, a positive direction:

> Yet you have made them a little lower than God,
>   and crowned them with glory and honor.
> You have given them dominion over the works of your hands;
>   you have put all things under their feet ... (Ps 8:5–6)

These are *bold* claims. Humans are a "little lower" than *elohim*. *Elohim* here could be translated as "God" (as in the NRSV) or as "the gods" (read: the lesser deities in the divine council) or as "angels" (which is the preferred translation in the Septuagint and the Targums and in the New Testament book of Hebrews). I tend to agree with the NRSV. Because the poem has so much thematic overlap with Genesis 1 and

---

[8] For this, and many other relatable images, see Eric Minton, *It's Not You, It's Everything: What Our Pain Reveals about the Anxious Pursuit of the Good Life* (Minneapolis: Broadleaf Books, 2022). This appears on page 46.
[9] Goldingay, *Psalms 1–41*, 158.

because *elohim* in Genesis 1 refers to God, the intonation of the term in Psalm 8 is probably the same. The psalmist, then, is claiming humans are a little lower than God.[10] They have been crowned with "glory and honor."[11]

This is not the "humans are guilty, tainted, and in need of redemption from birth" language some of us have adopted from our church experience. This is *kingly* language. Humanity has been "crowned." They have been given dominion or "made to rule." And here's the really surprising part, the language is *democratized*. The psalmist is claiming *all* humanity has been created in this way, all humanity has been entrusted with these tasks. Divinely granted authority, in other words, is not limited to kings. *All* humanity shares in this kingly function. Again, the thematic overlap with Genesis 1 is clear. The psalm places humanity in the role of "vice-regents."

Some readers, perhaps influenced by their predetermined theological commitments, want to challenge the psalm's claims on chronological grounds. Humans *may have been* this once. They were granted authority and entrusted to rule *originally*, but because of Adam and Eve's sin, they *aren't anymore*. But this isn't what the psalmist is saying. As one writer puts it, Psalm 8 has "unrestrained cultural optimism."[12] The poem, in its original context, was about humanity *back then* and humanity *now* and humanity *in the future*. Goldingay summarizes

---

[10] Even if alternatives are assumed, "gods" or "angels," the point is similar: humanity is important.

[11] Perhaps you're wondering why the author of Hebrews goes in a different direction (Hebrews 2:6–9) than what I am claiming for Psalm 8. Well, New Testament authors aren't always going after the "grammatical-historical" interpretation of their source texts in the Hebrew Bible. That's code for, sometimes they interpret the Hebrew Bible in an unexpected way to suit their own theological purposes. The author of Hebrews wants to connect the psalm to Jesus, but the psalm was not *originally* "Messianic." It was making an argument about humanity at large.

[12] Erhard S. Gerstenberger, *Psalms, Part 1 with an Introduction to Cultic Poetry* (The Forms of the Old Testament Literature; Grand Rapids, MI: Eerdmans, 1988), 70.

the psalmist's point, "What God intended humanity to be, God still intends humanity to be."[13]

The New Testament Authors Go in a Different Direction

I can't say if the author of Hebrews preferred a "Psalm 51 anthropology," but I can say they definitely didn't agree with a democratized, "*all humanity*" reading of Psalm 8. They write,

> "Now God did not subject the coming world, about which we are speaking, to angels. [Note: Hebrews has a lot to say about angels. Like everything else we've looked at, its cultural context is important.] But someone has testified somewhere,
>> What are human beings that you are mindful of them,
>>> or mortals, that you care for them?
>> You have made them for a little while lower [Note: that's different] than the angels;
>>> you have crowned them with glory and honor,
>>> subjecting all things under their feet.
> Now in subjecting all things to them, God left nothing outside their control. As it is, we do not yet see everything in subjection to them, *but we do see Jesus*, who for a little while was made lower than the angels, now crowned with glory and honor because of the suffering of death, so that by the grace of God he might taste death for everyone." (Heb 2:5–9)

Here's the point for the author of Hebrews: humanity had a job to do, but they failed. Jesus didn't. This interpretation—which features Jesus "fulfilling" the psalm—impacts the way many modern readers choose to interpret it. And I get it. If the author of Hebrews implies

---

[13] Goldingay, *Psalms 1–41*, 161.

that humanity blew it and then links the psalm to Jesus, we should too, right? I'm not so sure … and here's why.

M. Night Shyamalan, Jordan Peele, and Reading the Old Testament

We'll talk about what New Testament authors do with the Hebrew Bible in more detail in the next chapter. For now, we're on safe ground simply noting that the New Testament authors were not always (or even all that often) interested in preserving the "intended" meaning of the text. For them, the life, death, and resurrection of Jesus changed everything—including how they read, interpreted, and applied the Hebrew Bible.

Here's an analogy: what the New Testament authors did with the Hebrew Bible is like what we do when we watch something suspenseful like *The Sixth Sense* or *The Village* by M. Night Shyamalan or Jordan Peele's modern masterpiece, *Get Out*. The first time we see the film, we aren't sure what's happening. We're just hanging on for dear life, soaking in every minute of cinematic magic. Then, when the credits roll and everything has been revealed, we are floored because we did. not. see. *that ending* coming. When we re-watch these films, though, it's different. We know the ending, so it's hard *not* to see the plot unfolding on the screen in light of what we already know. Our knowledge of the end changes everything. We begin to see things we missed the first time, all the little clues from the writer/director that were buried. We might even see things that *weren't intended* and still make a connection to the end.

The New Testament authors had seen "the end of the movie," so to speak, and now, they couldn't *not* see it in their re-reading of the community's sacred texts. When they read the Hebrew Bible, they saw Jesus in places they didn't previously … or they put him in the story wherever they think there is a connection.

For example, for the author of Hebrews, Psalm 8 was no longer about humanity's vocation, regardless of what it meant in the past. That vocation was left unfulfilled until Jesus came along. The contrast, then, is between humanity's failure ("we *don't* see everything in subjection to *them*") and Jesus' success ("but *we do see Jesus*").

Paul offers a similar reading of Psalm 8 in 1 Corinthians 15:27. He, too, knows "the end of the movie," and he also identifies Jesus as the primary object under whose feet God has placed all things.

These readings aren't wrong. It would be silly of me to argue otherwise. But they are creative examples of good and accepted Jewish biblical interpretation. The writers are definitely taking some theological liberties with the psalm. They are re-reading it because they have been influenced by the person and work of Jesus. In its original context (and for centuries afterward and in some contexts, still today), the psalm was not looking forward to an idealized human figure who would one day "fulfill" the divine vocational calling. The psalmist was describing who humanity was created to be, what humanity was supposed to embody, the work humanity was given to do. And I'd propose, it still does, regardless of the author of Hebrews' or Paul's "Jesus" interpretation.

According to the psalmist, humanity was created a little lower than God, and was given a job to do—one that it *still* has. Christian readers, of course, can and should root this status and calling in the imitation of Christ. We should do what Jesus did, which, in this case, is what we were always expected to do! Jesus doesn't remove the obligation of the psalm. Rather, he provides a model for Christians to follow.

Reading the Hebrew Bible on Its Own Terms

I wonder what would happen if more of us read Psalm 8 like an ancient Israelite. Would we live into our calling? Would we be inspired to reclaim our divinely granted vocation? If we framed our theological understanding of creation and the world in an outlook of praise, would we see the grandeur in it all? Would it impact our care of the world? And if we moved beyond our felt insignificance/worthlessness/total depravity, would we be able to see ourselves as kings and queens?

However we choose to "apply" the passage, that is, whether we are impacted by it on a personal level or not, I think it's important to recover the theological undercurrent running throughout Psalm 8 *in its ancient context*. Neither the psalmist nor the community was compelled to see themselves as unworthy or guilty or shamed from birth. That wasn't part of their thinking. It doesn't even appear in the Hebrew Bible. Psalm 51, therefore, wasn't providing a universal anthropology. The psalmist of Psalm 8 and their community saw themselves as anointed image-bearers, entrusted with dominion and authority over creation. It may have been mind-boggling to consider, but the call was theirs for the taking.

To me, that's good news, and it's loaded with relevance for the way modern day readers of the psalm should live—for Christians, we're inclined to say, like Jesus, but might we also say, more broadly … like the queens and kings we were always intended to be.

Addendum: "I Am Fearfully and Wonderfully Made" (Psalm 139:13–14)

My sister became pregnant when she was 15. Like me, she was a Christian school kid, so her situation, if it became known, would create a scandal of massive proportions in our small community. She knew that, and as most people living in similar highly religious and shame-based contexts probably do, she considered getting an abortion. Ultimately, she decided not to. This decision had many consequences. She was expelled from our school. She became a byword for teenage sexual immorality and poor decision-making. My parents adjusted everything in their world to care for my sister, her boyfriend, and their new child, indelibly marking us as the family that "condones" sex outside of marriage and cohabitation.

When she told my parents, they reached out to a local pregnancy care center for guidance. An emerging relationship with the center would eventually result in a job for my mom and a board seat for my dad. It also resulted in my forced participation in the pregnancy center's abstinence-only skit troupe. Thankfully, I never had to perform any of the skits live, but my mom made me learn them so that I could, if the need arose, act out such classics as "Don't You Want to Chew My Bubble Gum?" (where the actor's sexuality was represented by a piece of Juicy Fruit that you definitely wanted to save for a special someone) and a couple of other human videos that involved a DC Talk soundtrack and using your hands to form a flying bird or a beating heart or some other symbol of your love. (If you did not grow up in the Christian sub-culture of the late 90s, I'm sure this sounds like a fever dream. You're not too far off, it was a weird time.)

I bring up my family's past because my Christian school, church, and the local pregnancy care center relied heavily upon Psalm 139:13–14 to buttress their commitment to a pro-life/anti-abortion ethical stance. In my mind, this is similar to the popular misreading of Psalm 51. The poetic lines in Psalm 139 are also read *universally*. The psalmist writes,

> For it was you who formed my inward parts;
>> you knit me together in my mother's womb.
> I praise you, for I am fearfully and wonderfully made.
>> Wonderful are your works;
>> that I know very well. (Ps 139:14–15)

The image at work here does indeed depict God's creative activity *in utero*. But it's not making a universal anthropological statement about when life begins. It's making a hyperbolic theological statement about the comprehensiveness of God's knowledge of, investment in, and care for the psalmist.

Set firmly within Book 5 of the Psalter, Psalm 139 provides an important counter-testimony for an exilic audience: the psalmist claims that they haven't been abandoned. They aren't alone. In fact, there is nowhere they can go to escape God's presence. God has been with them from the very beginning and will stay to the bitter end. To a displaced people, this message would have been life-giving. The psalmist claims, God cares, God is invested—always has been and always will be.

I wouldn't advise it, but if you absolutely have to choreograph a human video for some youth group kids, I say we start here.

CHAPTER SIXTEEN

The Psalms & Jesus

There are a couple of different ways we could approach a discussion on the Psalms and Jesus. One is to explore the record of Jesus' *use* of Psalms, which, according to the New Testament authors, is extensive. In fact, if you tally the number of citations of the Hebrew Bible made by Jesus in the New Testament, Psalms is quoted more than any other book.[1]

We've already discussed some of the difficulties associated with the *historical reconstruction* of Jesus' speech (Chapter Three). The Gospel authors were creatively and imaginatively shaping their retellings of the life, ministry, death, and resurrection of Jesus in order to suit their individual theological purposes. The goal was not transcribing Jesus' sermons word for word and then translating them accurately into a different language. The writers weren't preparing an objective historical report. Theirs was a *shaped* history, a *stylized* history, a *theologized* history.

Even though we are unable to verify the accuracy of the historical Jesus' spoken words, the recurring use of Psalms in these stories affirms that the book's contents held a special place in the hearts of his first-century Jewish audience. Further, as a first-century Jew himself, we are on safe ground concluding that Jesus would have known the Psalms, used the Psalms, and prayed and sung the Psalms. To place

---

[1] Here's a top 3 list: Psalms, Deuteronomy, and Isaiah.

the words of the Psalms' poems on his lips provides a compelling and perhaps surprising image of *how* and *what* Jesus might have prayed. As one of my former professors says, the Lord was *Christ's* shepherd, too.[2]

That's one way in. In this chapter, I'd like to expand on the work we began in the last chapter and explore how the New Testament authors use Psalms to help them tell the story of Jesus.

Reading the Psalms Christianly

Many Christians approach the content of the Hebrew Bible through a "Jesus lens." The fancy terminology for this approach is a Christocentric (Jesus is the focal point or center of the Hebrew Bible) or Christotelic (Jesus is the goal of the Hebrew Bible) hermeneutic. To revert to the analogy I used in the previous chapter, because we have seen the "end of the movie" (Jesus's death and resurrection), we are not able to *not* see him in the earlier portions of "the film" (the Hebrew Bible).

Approaching the Bible in this way, for Christians, is a time-honored approach that brings unity to the entire biblical narrative. And it has biblical precedent.

In Luke's Gospel, for example, Jesus commends the "Jesus lens" to two pilgrims on the road to Emmaus, who are traveling together after the traumatic events of Jesus' death and, unbeknownst to the two pilgrims, his resurrection. In response to their grief over these events, Jesus (whose identity was hidden from them) says, "Oh, how foolish you are, and how slow of heart to believe all that the prophets have declared! Was it not necessary that the Messiah should suffer these things and then enter into his glory?" (Luke 24:25–27). In other words, Jesus is saying, everything that has happened here was all *in there*. You should

---

[2] See Douglas J. Green, "The Lord is Christ's Shepherd: Psalm 23 as Messianic Prophecy," in *Eyes to See, Ears to Hear: Essays in Memory of J. Alan Groves*, Peter Enns, Douglas J. Green, and Michael B. Kelly, eds. (Phillipsburg, NJ; P&R Publishing, 2010), 33–46.

have picked up on it! To demonstrate his point, he starts teaching the Hebrew Bible. Luke says, "beginning with Moses and all the prophets," Jesus "interpreted to them the things about himself in *all the scriptures*" (v. 27).

In the next vignette, the same post-resurrection Jesus appears to his disciples. After eating a piece of broiled fish to prove that he was not an apparition (vv. 42–43), it says that he taught them "that everything written about me in the law of Moses, the prophets, *and the psalms* must be fulfilled" (v. 44). Again, the claim from Luke is that the end of the movie was foretold in some way in its earlier scenes.

Based on these texts, the resulting hermeneutical approach—"Jesus as the fulfillment/focal point/goal"—provides an appropriate Christian interpretive lens for a reading of the Hebrew Bible, Psalms included. As we have already seen with the author of Hebrews' re-reading of Psalm 8, the New Testament authors put it into practice. The implication is, Psalms was not just a collection of poems that Jesus may have read or cited or prayed, it was *about Jesus* in some way.

Granted, this is applied with greater ease to certain psalms, especially those dubbed the "messianic psalms." Psalm 2 is a good example. The psalmist writes,

> "I will tell of the decree of the LORD:
>> He said to me, 'You are my son;
>> today I have begotten you.'" (v. 7)

In its original context, the anointing (v. 2) and sonship of this character are kingly motifs. By the time the Psalter was completed, however, human kings were a thing of the past, which encouraged some to read this passage "prophetically." An idealized Davidic king—the anointed son—would come one day. The term for anointed, in fact, can also mean "messiah."

For Christians, the ties to Jesus are clear. Peter famously confesses Jesus as "the Christ," which in Greek is linked with "the Lord's anointed" or "messiah" (Matt 16:13–20). The familial attribution, "my son," also speaks of Jesus. New Testament authors connect these dots in the retelling of Paul's sermon in Acts 13 (v. 33), in the book of Hebrews (1:5; 5:5), and in 2 Peter (1:17). Declarations of divine sonship are also featured in pivotal moments in Jesus's life. For example, in Matthew's story of Jesus's baptism, the skies open up, a dove descends, and a divine voice proclaims, "This is my son" (Matt 3:17). In Matthew's retelling of the Transfiguration, the divine voice once again identifies Jesus with the words, "This is my son" (17:5). In Mark's Gospel, a centurion who witnessed Jesus' crucifixion and death claimed, "Truly this man was God's Son!" (Mark 15:39).

Applying this hermeneutic to Psalms, it's easy to see why Christians would be led from Psalm 2 to Jesus. According to Christian theology, Jesus is the rightful, expected Davidic king. But Psalm 2 doesn't exist simply to bear witness to Jesus. It's not "messianic" in the sense that it was written to point centuries ahead to Jesus. The psalm had (and has) a life of its own apart from this very Christian interpretation. Think of the entire Jewish interpretive enterprise! To claim Jesus is the text's single goal diminishes an entire tradition of biblical interpretation and verges on supersessionism—the dismissing/diminishing of Jewish tradition by claiming Christian theology as its "fulfillment."

There is a tension, then, in reading the Psalms "messianically." Psalm 2 wasn't originally intended as a prophetic utterance predicting the life, death, and/or resurrection of Jesus. The New Testament authors read him back in, as many Christians continue to do today.

The "Fulfillment" of Psalm 22

Psalm 22 offers another interesting example. For those familiar with the New Testament, the opening colon of this lament psalm is best known as Jesus' cry of divine abandonment from the cross,

"My God, my God, why have you forsaken me?" (v. 1)

In his attributed citation of the psalm, Jesus, of course, was not attempting to "fulfill" it, as if the psalm was originally produced for use in this climactic moment centuries later. It is much easier to think that *if* Jesus cited the psalm, it was because he was so saturated in sacred Scripture, he would have voiced this very appropriate psalm at this very appropriate moment of his life.

It is also possible that the Gospel authors placed *this particular psalm* on Jesus' lips to aid their *(shaped, stylized, theological)* retelling of his story. In fact, some Gospel authors used the entirety of Psalm 22 to frame their version of Jesus' final hours, not just his cry on the cross. To demonstrate this, I will include relevant lines from Psalm 22 and connect them with the narrative from the Gospel of Matthew.

But I am a worm, and not human;
    scorned by others, and despised by the people.
All who see me mock at me;
    they make mouths at me, ***they shake their heads*** … (Ps 22:6–7)

> Then two bandits were crucified with him, one on his right and one on his left. Those who passed by derided him, ***shaking their heads*** and saying … (Matt 27:38–39)

Commit your cause to the Lord; ***let him deliver—***
let him rescue the one in whom he delights! (Ps 22:8)

> In the same way the chief priests also, along with the scribes and elders, were mocking him, saying, "He saved others; he cannot save himself. He is the King of Israel; ***let him come down from the cross now***, and we will believe in him. He trusts in God; ***let God deliver him now***, if he wants to; for he said, 'I am God's Son.'" The bandits who were crucified with him also taunted him in the same way.
> (Matt 27:41–44)

For dogs are all around me;
  a company of evildoers encircles me. (Ps 22:16a)

> So when Pilate saw that he could do nothing, but rather
> that a *riot was beginning*, he took some water and washed
> his hands *before the crowd*, saying, "I am innocent of
> this man's blood; see to it yourselves." Then the people as
> a whole answered, "His blood be on us and on our chil-
> dren!"…Then the soldiers of the governor took Jesus into
> the governor's headquarters, and *they gathered the whole
> cohort around him*. (Matt 27:24–25, 27)

My hands and feet have shriveled;
  I can count all my bones. (Ps 22:16b–17a)

> So he released Barabbas for them; and after *flogging* Jesus
> [which would have, theoretically exposed his bones], he
> handed him over to be crucified. (Matt 27:26)

They stare and gloat over me … (Ps 22:17b)

> They stripped him and put a scarlet robe on him, and after
> twisting some thorns into a crown, they put it on his head.
> They put a reed in his right hand and knelt before him *and
> mocked him*, saying, "Hail, King of the Jews!" They spat
> on him, and took the reed and struck him on the head.
> *After mocking him*, they stripped him of the robe and put
> his own clothes on him. Then they led him away to crucify
> him. (Matt 27:28–31)

they *divide my clothes* among themselves,
  and for my clothing they *cast lots*. (Ps 22:18)

And when they had crucified him, ***they divided his clothes*** among themselves ***by casting lots***…(Matt 27:35)

My God, my God, why have you forsaken me?
Why are you so far from helping me, from the words of my groaning?
O my God, I cry by day, but you do not answer;
and by night, but find no rest. (Ps 22:1–2)

From noon on, darkness came over the whole land until three in the afternoon. And about three o'clock Jesus cried with a loud voice, "Eli, Eli, lema sabachthani?" that is, ***"My God, my God, why have you forsaken me?"*** (Matt 27:45–46)

Clearly, some of the connections above are more thematic than verbal, particularly the bits about "counting my bones" or enemies "staring and gloating," but the images are certainly there. At other times, though, the overlap between the two texts is uncanny. The author of Matthew, seemingly, is inspired by the content of the psalm and has shaped it, stylized it, theologized it, for use in his retelling of Jesus' death, with the final scene coalescing with Jesus' citation of Psalm 22 on the cross.[3]

Using the Jesus Lens

Matthew's use of Psalm 22 isn't *prophetic*, at least not in the sense that the psalm was viewed as something to be fulfilled. It's an example of how Jesus, when viewed as the end of the movie, shaped the New

---

[3] I am not trying to make a stance on Matthew's source material. He may have been borrowing from Mark's Gospel. A similar tradition linking Psalm 22 and the end of Jesus's life emerges there as well.

Testament authors' reading of the Hebrew Bible. Read on its own, Psalm 22 is a lament psalm. The New Testament authors may have re-imagined it to explain the deep suffering Jesus experienced on the cross, but its application is not limited to Jesus. The New Testament authors' use of the psalm, therefore, is similar to the editor's addition of psalm titles: it's an editorial comment urging readers to see Jesus (or David) in the psalm, but they need not be constrained by such identifications.

In a sense, you could say that the entire Psalter is "messianic," meaning, Jesus the Christ (Messiah) used it, sang it, prayed it, that he experienced the breadth of the experiences contained in it, that he celebrated and proclaimed its theology, that he lived out the ethic it proposes. As Christians, you could also say that Psalms speaks of Jesus, of his life, death, and resurrection, though here, I would be careful to admit this is a reading *in*, albeit a good one. Individual psalms have a context and purpose all their own, one worthy of appreciation, which is what we've been doing throughout this book.[4]

---

[4] For a good introduction to this sort of thinking, see John Goldingay, *Do We Need the New Testament? Letting the Old Testament Speak for Itself* (Downers Grove, IL: IVP Academic, 2015).

Conclusion

We made it! Before you go and update your Goodreads with a nice five-star review, let's take a breath. This "ending" is really only the beginning when it comes to Psalms. Throughout this book, I've tried to show that reading a psalm demands some awareness of the history of the book—its formation, its current shape, the genre analysis and literary artistry of the poetry, an acknowledgement of its oldness and ambiguity, and its potential use in worship. Because the emotions on display in Psalms and the experiences the psalmists describe are sometimes immediately relatable, we don't always think through these important background issues. We equate ourselves a little too quickly with the unnamed "I" in the psalm. Failure to engage with the introductory issues, however, will make it difficult for us to fully assess what is going on in a psalm (and, if so inclined, how we might use it ourselves). I've given you some of the raw tools, now it's up to you to apply them and add to them.

Regarding the book's theology, I have provided only a small sampling of the (many) culturally-embedded theological snapshots in Psalms. Hopefully, we have seen enough to be encouraged to read each psalm on its own terms, without importing either our own theological commitments or those of the New Testament authors (!) back onto the text. I have also warned against importing the theological commitments of *other psalms* onto the psalm in front of us. The book is diverse in its outlook. As Brueggemann suggests, dialogue is a good word to guide our reading of Psalms.

I'm biased, but I think this is important work, and it's not for the faint of heart. Sometimes when we dig into the past, we learn new things—things that may upset what we once thought, maybe even what we once held dear. But a reading of Psalms that is historically and contextually informed, and theologically aware, can yield many benefits. It can shed light on misreadings, limited readings, over-readings, and readings with a misplaced focus. More positively, it can enhance our view of what a psalm is saying. I know from experience that it isn't easy to be challenged, but I hope the previous pages have helped you see there is often more to the story than what we originally thought. Personally, I have found so much life in the process of unlearning and relearning, whether it's inquiries like, did David write Psalms, or how many gods *did* the ancient Israelites believe in, or is a "Jesus reading" of the Hebrew Bible the only reading. I hope that might be true for you, too.

The book of Psalms has been described as the "daily lifeblood" of the Jewish and Christian community. I'm not entirely sure how true that is today, but I hope that Psalms now feels a little less intimidating, a little less "crazy," "violent" or "old," and that our response to it is a little less, "Psalms is the greatest thing ever, I have no questions or reservations whatsoever" or, alternatively, "I hate Psalms, it's stupid."

This, too, is a beginning. And I think it is one we can build on.

Things for Normal People to Read (Or Not ... No Judgment)

Introductory Works on Psalms

deClaissé-Walford, Nancy L. *Introduction to the Psalms: A Song from Ancient Israel.* Danvers, MA: Chalice Press, 2004.

Jacobson, Rolf A. and Karl N. Jacobson. *Invitation to the Psalms: A Reader's Guide for Discovery and Engagement.* Grand Rapids, MI: Baker Academic, 2013.

Introductory Works on Biblical Hebrew Poetry

Alter, Robert. *The Art of Biblical Poetry.* Rev. Ed. New York: Basic Books, 2011.

Kugel, James L. *The Idea of Biblical Poetry: Parallelism and Its History.* Baltimore: The Johns Hopkins University Press, 1981.

Petersen, David L. and Kent Harold Richards. *Interpreting Hebrew Poetry.* Guides to Biblical Scholarship. Minneapolis: Fortress Press, 1992.

Psalms Commentaries

Brueggemann, Walter and William H. Bellinger, Jr. *Psalms*. New Cambridge Bible Commentary. New York: Cambridge University Press, 2014.

deClaissé-Walford, Nancy L., Rolf A. Jacobson, and Beth LaNeel Tanner. *The Book of Psalms*. The New International Commentary on the Old Testament. Grand Rapids, MI: Eerdmans, 2014.

Goldingay, John. *Psalms*. 3 vols. Baker Commentary on the Old Testament Wisdom and Psalms. Grand Rapids, MI: Baker Academic, 2006–08.

McCann, J. Clinton, Jr. "The Book of Psalms." Pages 273–729 in Vol. 3 of *The New Interpreter's Bible*. Edited by Leander E. Keck. Nashville: Abingdon, 2015.

Theology of Psalms

Brueggemann, Walter. *The Psalms and the Life of Faith*. Edited by Patrick D. Miller. Minneapolis: Fortress Press, 1995.

McCann, J. Clinton, Jr. *A Theological Introduction to the Book of Psalms: The Psalms as Torah*. Nashville: Abingdon, 1993.

Wenham, Gordon J. *Psalms as Torah: Reading Biblical Song Ethically*. Studies in Theological Interpretation. Grand Rapids, MI: Baker Academic, 2012.

Zenger, Erich. *A God of Vengeance?: Understanding the Psalms of Divine Wrath*. Translated by Linda M. Maloney. Louisville: Westminster John Knox Press, 1994.

Acknowledgments

The Bible for Normal People podcast has a recurring series where Pete "ruins" books of the Bible. Well, he ruins people, too. I'm one of them, and I owe him a debt of gratitude. For many years, my reading of the Bible had no nuance. It was flat. It was limited. It was *safe*. I would regularly contort it to meet the demands of my community's accepted theology. Then I met Pete and a handful of other gifted teachers of the Bible, who opened my eyes to new possibilities. Pete and this cadre lovingly ruined my view of the Bible, but in the best way. (Alright, Pete wasn't exactly "loving" in the seminary classroom, but you get the point.) I can say with full assurance, I wouldn't be who I am without any of them.

In addition to the aforementioned Pete Enns, this list of influential teachers and mentors includes my doctoral supervisor, the one and only, John Goldingay, Doug Green, the late Al Groves, Chris Hays, Les Hicks, Mike Kelly, TL3, Jim McGahey, and many others. I am thankful for their example and their commitment to intellectual honesty.

I would also like to thank The Restoration Project, a small Cooperative Baptist Fellowship church in Salisbury, Maryland. This community provides my working template for "normal people"—even though, who are we kidding, none of us are exactly "normal." Special shoutout to its leaders for allowing me the time to be involved in projects like this: Suzi, Tessa, Christi, Amanda, and Laura. You're the best. Hand to the plow, people. We have work to do.

Other friends, who have provided insight and encouragement include Dr. Jennifer Garcia Bashaw, Jonathan Bow, Eric Minton, the trailblazer and trend-setter, Jared Byas, and all those who have read/commented on/critiqued portions of this book before it went into print: Christi Engle, Melissa Marsh, Jeff Marshall, Jeff Scott, and Dr. Sara Wells. Finally, many thanks to Lauren O'Connell—editor extraordinaire. She made my writing much better and saved me many times from inaccuracy and certain embarrassment.

Much love to my parents for being all supportive and stuff, my sister, Erica, for being a badass, and her husband, Jim.

Finally, to my crew—Kate, Abe, and Jude. Everything I do is for you. *Always.* I love you all.

About this Book

About the Author

Joshua T. James (PhD, Fuller Theological Seminary) is one of the pastors of The Restoration Project in Salisbury, Maryland. He also serves as an "Affiliate Assistant Professor of Old Testament" at his alma mater, which is a fancy way of saying, he's very very part-time. Josh lives on the Eastern Shore of Maryland with his wife, Kate, their two sons, Abe and Jude, and Porter, a beagle who is endlessly plotting his great escape.

Behind the Scenes

Publishing Director Lauren O'Connell
Cover Design Tessa McKay Stultz
Layout Designer Ania Lenihan

Special thanks to the eagle-eyed members of our Society of Normal People community who read through the final draft of the manuscript and provided feedback, caught spelling errors, and generally ensured we don't look like fools: Michael Burdge, Julia Clark, Phillip Gibson, Greg Glidden, Bob and Yvonna Graham, Rex Gray, Michael Greene, Charlene Holloway, William F. Kerwin, John Shumate, Peter Wall and Blake M. Wilson. We couldn't do what we do without you.

Enjoyed this Book?

To continue the conversation, head over to thebiblefornormalpeople. com where you can:

- Listen to the only God-ordained podcasts on the internet: The Bible for Normal People and Faith for Normal People.
- Join our community for members-only content and perks, and journey alongside others who are asking the tough questions.
- Read hundreds of articles from biblical scholars, theologians and practitioners.
- Buy even more books and exclusive B4NP merch.
- Enroll in one of our online courses and deep dive into your area of interest.

Or follow us on Facebook and Instagram (@thebiblefornormalpeople) for more Bible for Normal People content.

Printed in the USA
CPSIA information can be obtained
at www.ICGtesting.com
LVHW052023070923
757553LV00005B/180